THE COVERLEY PAPERS

Illustrated by Gordon Ross

*An Invitation from Sir Roger
to pass away a Month in the Country*

THE
Sir Roger de Coverley
PAPERS

BY JOSEPH ADDISON, RICHARD STEELE

AND EUSTACE BUDGELL

from THE SPECTATOR, *London: 1711-1712*

With Some Prefatory Notes by W. M. Thackeray, and

Illustrations Drawn for this Edition by Gordon Ross

NEW YORK: THE HERITAGE PRESS

*The special contents of this edition are copyright, 1945,
by The George Macy Companies, Inc.*

THE TABLE OF CONTENTS

Some Prefatory Notes by W. M. Thackeray
CHAPTER   Page
    The Author's Preface 3
    I. Sir Roger and the Club 9
    II. Coverley Hall 17
    III. The Coverley Household 22
    IV. The Coverley Guest 27
    V. The Coverley Lineage 32
    VI. The Coverley Ghost 38
    VII. The Coverley Sabbath 42
    VIII. Sir Roger in Love 47
    IX. The Coverley Œconomy 55
    X. The Coverley Hunt 60
    XI. The Coverley Witch 68
    XII. A Coverley Love Match 73
    XIII. The Coverley Etiquette 79
    XIV. The Coverley Ducks 83
    XV. Sir Roger on the Bench 88
    XVI. A Story of an Heir 94

Chapter	Page
XVII. Sir Roger and Party Spirit	101
XVIII. On Gipseys in General	107
XIX. A Summons to London	110
XX. Farewell to Coverley Hall	115
XXI. Sir Roger in London	121
XXII. Sir Roger in Westminster Abbey	127
XXIII. Sir Roger at the Playhouse	133
XXIV. Sir Roger at Vaux-hall	139
XXV. Sir Roger, The Widow, Will Honeycomb, and Milton	143
XXVI. Sir Roger Passeth Away	148
The Translations of the Mottoes	153
Some Notes	156

A LIST OF THE PLATES

"An Invitation from Sir Roger to pass away a Month in the Country" . *Frontispiece*

Sir Joseph Addison . . . . . . *Title page*

"A very venerable Man of good Sense and some Learning" . . . *facing page* 20

Will Wimble 28

"I have been Fool enough to carve her Name" 48

Cheering the Hounds 64

The Perverse Widow 76

Tom Touchy, a Fellow famous for taking the Law of every Body 92

The invidious Behaviour of Military Men 116

Sir Roger at the Play 132

Sir Roger Reflects that the Thames is the noblest River 140

"She never saw a Gentleman with such a spindle Pair of legs as Mr. Honeycomb" 144

SOME PREFATORY NOTES
by William Makepeace Thackeray

I

WHAT do we look for in studying the history of a past age? Is it to learn the political transactions and characters of the leading public men? Is it to make ourselves acquainted with the life and being of the time? If we set out with the former grave purpose, where is the truth, and who believes that he has it entire? What character of what great man is known to you? You can but make guesses as to character more or less happy. In common life don't you often judge and misjudge a man's whole conduct, setting out from a wrong impression? The tone of a voice, a word said in joke, a trifle in behaviour—the cut of his hair or the tie of his neckcloth may disfigure him in your eyes, or poison your good opinion; or at the end of years of intimacy it may be your closest friend says something, reveals something which had previously been a secret, which alters all your views about him, and shows that he has been acting on quite a different motive to that which you fancied you knew. And if it is so with those you know, how much more with those you don't know?

I doubt all autobiographies I ever read; except those, perhaps, of Mr. Robinson Crusoe, Mariner, and writers of his class. *These* have no object in setting themselves right with the public or their own consciences; these have no motive for concealment or half-truths; these call for no more confidence than I can cheerfully give, and do not force me

The Coverley Papers

to tax my credulity or to fortify it by evidence. I take up a volume of Doctor Smollett, or a volume of the *Spectator*, and say the fiction carries a greater amount of truth in solution than the volume which purports to be all true. Out of the fictitious book I get the expression of the life of the time; of the manners, of the movement, the dress, the pleasures, the laughter, the ridicules of society—the old times live again, and I travel in the old country of England. Can the heaviest historian do more for me?

As we read in these delightful essays the past age returns, the England of our ancestors is revivified. The Maypole rises in the Strand again in London; the churches are thronged with daily worshippers; the beaux are gathering in the coffee-houses; the gentry are going to the Drawing-room; the ladies are thronging to the toy-shops; the chairmen are jostling in the streets; the footmen are running with links before the chariots, or fighting round the theatre doors. In the country I see the young Squire riding to Eton with his servants behind him, and Will Wimble, the friend of the family, to see him safe. To make that journey from the Squire's and back, Will is a week on horseback. The coach takes five days between London and Bath. The judges and the bar ride the circuit. If my Lady comes to town in her post-chariot, her people carry pistols to fire a salute on Captain Macheath if he should appear, and her couriers ride ahead to prepare apartments for her at the great caravanserais on the road; Boniface receives her under the creaking sign of the "Bell" or the "Ram," and he and his chamberlains bow her up the great stair to the state apartments, whilst her carriage rumbles into the courtyard, where the "Exeter Fly" is housed that performs the journey in eight days, God willing, having achieved its daily flight of twenty miles, and landed its passengers for supper

Some Prefatory Notes

and sleep. The curate is taking his pipe in the kitchen, where the Captain's man—having hung up his master's half-pike—is at his bacon and eggs, bragging of Ramillies and Malplaquet to the townsfolk, who have their club in the chimney-corner. The Captain is ogling the chambermaid in the wooden gallery, or bribing her to know who is the pretty young mistress that has come in the coach. The pack-horses are in the great stable, and the drivers and ostlers carousing in the tap. And in Mrs. Landlady's bar, over a glass of strong waters, sits a gentleman of military appearance, who travels with pistols, as all the rest of the world does, and has a rattling grey mare in the stables which will be saddled and away with its owner half an hour before the "Fly" sets out on its last day's flight. And some five miles on the road, as the "Exeter Fly" comes jingling and creaking onwards, it will suddenly be brought to a halt by a gentleman on a grey mare, with a black vizard on his face, who thrusts a long pistol into the coach window, and bids the company to hand out their purses. . . . Contrast these with the writings of our present humourists! Compare those morals and ours—those manners and ours!

We can't tell—you would not bear to be told—the whole truth regarding those men and manners. You could no more suffer in a British drawing-room, under the reign of Queen Victoria, a fine gentleman or fine lady of Queen Anne's time, or hear what they heard and said, than you would receive an ancient Briton. It is as one reads about savages, that one contemplates the wild ways, the barbarous feasts, the terrific pastimes, of the men of pleasure of that age. We have our fine gentlemen, and our "fast men"; permit me to give you an idea of two noblemen of Queen Anne's days.

II

Kind, just, serene, impartial, his fortitude not tried beyond easy endurance, his affections not much used, for his books were his family, and his society was in public; admirably wiser, wittier, calmer, and more instructed than almost every man with whom he met, how could Joseph Addison suffer, desire, admire, feel much? I may expect a child to admire me for being taller or writing more cleverly than she; but how can I ask my superior to say that I am a wonder when he knows better than I? In Addison's days you could scarcely show him a literary performance, a sermon, or a poem, or a piece of literary criticism, but he felt he could do better. His justice must have made him indifferent. He didn't praise, because he measured his compeers by a higher standard than common people have. How was he who was so tall to look up to any but the loftiest genius? He must have stooped to put himself on a level with most men.

Addison's father was a clergyman of good repute in Wiltshire, and rose in the Church. His famous son never lost his clerical training and scholastic gravity, and was called "a parson in a tye-wig" in London afterwards at a time when tye-wigs were only worn by the laity, and the fathers of theology did not think it decent to appear except in a full bottom. Having been at school at Salisbury, and the Charterhouse in 1687, when he was fifteen years old, he went to Queen's College, Oxford, where he speedily began to distinguish himself by the making of Latin verses. The beautiful and fanciful poem of "The Pigmies and the Cranes" is still read by lovers of that sort of exercise; and verses are extant in honour of King William, by which it appears that it was the loyal youth's custom to toast that sovereign in bumpers of purple Lyæus: many more works

Some Prefatory Notes

are in the Collection, including one on the Peace of Ryswick, in 1697, which was so good that Montague got him a pension of £300 a year, on which Addison set out on his travels.

During his ten years at Oxford, Addison had deeply imbued himself with the Latin poetical literature and had these poets at his fingers' ends when he travelled in Italy. His patron went out of office, and his pension was unpaid: and hearing that this great scholar, now eminent and known to the literati of Europe (the great Boileau, upon perusal of Mr. Addison's elegant hexameters, was first made aware that England was not altogether a barbarous nation)—hearing that the celebrated Mr. Addison, of Oxford, proposed to travel as governor to a young gentleman on the grand tour, the great Duke of Somerset proposed to Mr. Addison to accompany his son, Lord Hertford.

Mr. Addison was delighted to be of use to his Grace, and his Lordship his Grace's son, and expressed himself ready to set forth.

His Grace the Duke of Somerset now announced to one of the most famous scholars of Oxford and Europe that it was his gracious intention to allow my Lord Hertford's tutor one hundred guineas per annum. Mr. Addison wrote back that his services were his Grace's, but he by no means found his account in the recompense for them. The negotiation was broken off. They parted with a profusion of *congées* on one side and the other.

Addison remained abroad for some time, living in the best society of Europe. How could he do otherwise? He must have been one of the finest gentlemen the world ever saw: at all moments of life serene and courteous, cheerful and calm. He could scarcely ever have had a degrading thought. He might have omitted a virtue or two, or many,

The Coverley Papers

but could not have committed many faults for which he need blush or turn pale. When warmed into confidence, his conversation appears to have been so delightful that the greatest wits sat rapt and charmed to listen to him. No man bore poverty and narrow fortune with a more lofty cheerfulness. His letters to his friends at this period of his life, when he had lost his Government pension and given up his college chances, are full of courage and a gay confidence and philosophy: and they are none the worse in my eyes, and I hope not in those of his last and greatest biographer (though Mr. Macaulay is bound to own and lament a certain weakness for wine, which the great and good Joseph Addison notoriously possessed, in common with countless gentlemen of his time), because some of the letters are written when his honest hand was shaking a little in the morning after libations to purple Lyæus over-night. He was fond of drinking the healths of his friends. A better and more Christian man scarcely ever breathed than Joseph Addison. If he had not that little weakness for wine—why, we could scarcely have found a fault with him, and could not have liked him as we do.

At thirty-three years of age, this most distinguished wit, scholar, and gentleman was without a profession and an income. His book of "Travels" had failed: his "Dialogues on Medals" had had no particular success: his Latin verses, even though reported the best since Virgil, or Statius at any rate, had not brought him a Government place, and Addison was living up three shabby pair of stairs in the Haymarket (in a poverty over which old Samuel Johnson rather chuckles), when in these shabby rooms an emissary from Government and Fortune came and found him. A poem was wanted about the Duke of Marlborough's victory of Blenheim. Would Mr. Addison write one? Mr.

Some Prefatory Notes

Boyle, afterwards Lord Carlton, took back the reply to the Lord Treasurer Godolphin, that Mr. Addison would. When the poem had reached a certain stage, it was carried to Godolphin. That angel, that good angel, flew off with Mr. Addison, and landed him in the place of Commissioner of Appeals—*vice* Mr. Locke providentially promoted. In the following year Mr. Addison went to Hanover with Lord Halifax, and the year after was made Under-Secretary of State. O angel visits! you come "few and far between" to literary gentlemen's lodgings! your wings seldom quiver at second-floor windows now!

But it is not for his reputation as the great author of "Cato" and the "Campaign," or for his merits as Secretary of State, or for his rank and high distinction as my Lady Warwick's husband, or for his eminence as an Examiner of political questions on the Whig side, or a Guardian of British liberties, that we admire Joseph Addison. It is as a Tatler of small talk and a Spectator of mankind, that we cherish and love him, and owe as much pleasure to him as to any human being that ever wrote. He came in that artificial age, and began to speak with his noble, natural voice. He came, the gentle satirist, who hit no unfair blow; the kind judge who castigated only in smiling.

Addison wrote his papers as gaily as if he was going out for a holiday. When Steele's *Tatler* first began his prattle, Addison, then in Ireland, caught at his friend's notion, poured in paper after paper, and contributed the stores of his mind, the sweet fruits of his reading, the delightful gleanings of his daily observation, with a wonderful profusion, and as it seemed, an almost endless fecundity. He was six-and-thirty years old: full and ripe. He had not worked crop after crop from his brain, manuring hastily, subsoiling indifferently, cutting and sowing and cutting again, like other luckless cultivators of letters. He had not done much as yet: a few Latin poems—graceful prolusions; a polite book of travels; a dissertation on medals, not very deep; four acts of a tragedy, a great classical exercise; and the "Campaign," a large prize poem that won an enormous prize. But with his friend's discovery of the *Tatler*, Addison's calling was found, and the most delightful talker in the world began to speak. He does not go very deep: let gentlemen of a profound genius, critics accustomed to the plunge of the bathos, console themselves by thinking that he *couldn't* go very deep. There are no traces of suffering in his writing. He was so good, so honest, so healthy, so cheerfully selfish, if I must use the word. There is no deep sentiment. I doubt, until after his marriage, perhaps, whether he ever lost his night's rest or his day's tranquillity about any woman in his life; whereas poor Dick Steele had capacity enough to melt, and to languish, and to sigh, and to cry his honest old eyes out, for a dozen. His writings do not show insight into or reverence for the love of women, which I take to be, one the consequence of the other. He walks about the world watching their pretty humours, fashions, follies, flirtations, rivalries: and noting them with the most charming archness. He sees them in public, in the theatre, or the assembly, or the puppet-show; or at the toy-shop higgling for gloves and lace; or at the auction, battling together over a blue porcelain dragon, or a darling monster in Japan; or at church, eyeing the width of their rival's hoops, or the breadth of their laces, as they sweep down the aisles. Or he looks out of his window at the "Garter" in Saint James's Street, at Ardelia's coach, as she blazes to the drawing-room with her coronet and six footmen; and remembering that her father was a Turkey merchant in the City, cal-

Some Prefatory Notes

culates how many sponges went to purchase her earring, and how many drums of figs to build her coach-box; or he demurely watches behind a tree in Spring Garden as Saccharissa (whom he knows under her mask) trips out of her chair to the alley where Sir Fopling is waiting. He sees only the public life of women. Addison was one of the most resolute club-men of his day. He passed many hours daily in those haunts. Besides drinking—which, alas! is past praying for—you must know it, he owned, too, ladies, that he indulged in that odious practice of smoking. Poor fellow! He was a man's man, remember. The only woman he *did* know, he didn't write about. I take it there would not have been much humour in that story.

He likes to go and sit in the smoking-room at the "Grecian," or the "Devil"; to pace 'Change and the Mall —to mingle in that great club of the world—sitting alone in it somehow: having good-will and kindness for every single man and woman in it—having need of some habit and custom binding him to some few; never doing any man a wrong (unless it be a wrong to hint a little doubt about a man's parts, and to damn him with faint praise); and so he looks on the world and plays with the ceaseless humours of all of us—laughs the kindest laugh—points our neighbour's foible or eccentricity out to us with the most good-natured smiling confidence; and then, turning over his shoulder, whispers our foibles to our neighbour. What would Sir Roger de Coverley be without his follies and his charming little brain-cracks? If the good knight did not call out to the people sleeping in church, and say "Amen" with such a delightful pomposity; if he did not make a speech in the assize-court *à propos de bottes,* and merely to show his dignity to Mr. Spectator: if he did not mistake Madam Doll Tearsheet for a lady of quality in Temple

Garden: if he were wiser than he is: if he had not his humour to salt his life, and were but a mere English gentleman and game-preserver—of what worth were he to us? We love him for his vanities as much as his virtues. What is ridiculous is delightful in him; we are so fond of him because we laugh at him so. And out of that laughter, and out of that sweet weakness, and out of those harmless eccentricities and follies, and out of that touched brain, and out of that honest manhood and simplicity—we get a result of happiness, goodness, tenderness, pity, piety; such as, if my audience will think their reading and hearing over, doctors and divines but seldom have the fortune to inspire. And why not? Is the glory of Heaven to be sung only by gentlemen in black coats? Must the truth be only expounded in gown and surplice, and out of those two vestments can nobody preach it? Commend me to this dear preacher without orders—this parson in the tye-wig. When this man looks from the world, whose weaknesses he describes so benevolently, up to the Heaven which shines over us all, I can hardly fancy a human face lighted up with a more serene rapture: a human intellect thrilling with a purer love and adoration than Joseph Addison's.

When he turns to Heaven, a Sabbath comes over that man's mind: and his face lights up from it with a glory of thanks and prayer. His sense of religion stirs through his whole being. In the fields, in the town: looking at the birds in the trees: at the children in the streets: in the morning or in the moonlight: over his books in his own room: in a happy party at a country merry-making or a town assembly, good-will and peace to God's creatures, and love and awe of Him who made them, fill his pure heart and shine from his kind face. If Swift's life was the most wretched, I think Addison's was one of the most enviable. A life pros-

Some Prefatory Notes

perous and beautiful—a calm death—an immense fame and affection afterwards for his happy and spotless name.

III

Shortly before the Boyne was fought, and young Swift had begun to make acquaintance with English Court manners and English servitude in Sir William Temple's family, another Irish youth was brought to learn his humanities at the old school of Charterhouse, near Smithfield; to which foundation he had been appointed by James Duke of Ormond, a governor of the House, and a patron of the lad's family. The boy was an orphan, and described, twenty years after, with a sweet pathos and simplicity, some of the earliest recollections of a life which was destined to be chequered by a strange variety of good and evil fortune.

I am afraid no good report could be given by his masters and ushers of that thick-set, square-faced, black-eyed, soft-hearted little Irish boy. He was very idle. He was whipped deservedly a great number of times. Though he had very good parts of his own, he got other boys to do his lessons for him, and only took just as much trouble as should enable him to scuffle through his exercises, and by good fortune escape the flogging-block.

Besides being very kind, lazy, and good-natured, this boy went invariably into debt with the tart-woman; ran out of bounds, and entered into pecuniary, or rather promissory, engagements with the neighbouring lollipop vendors and piemen—exhibited an early fondness and capacity for drinking mum and sack, and borrowed from all his comrades who had money to lend.

Almost every gentleman who does me the honour to read me will remember that the very greatest character which he has seen in the course of his life, and the person to whom he has looked up with the greatest wonder and reverence, was the head boy at his school. The schoolmaster himself hardly inspires such an awe. The head boy construes as well as the schoolmaster himself. When he begins to speak the hall is hushed, and every little boy listens. He writes off copies of Latin verses as melodiously as Virgil. He is good-natured, and, his own masterpieces achieved, pours out other copies of verses for other boys with an astonishing ease and fluency; the idle ones only trembling lest they should be discovered on giving in their exercises, and whipped because their poems were too good.

Dick Steele, the Charterhouse gownboy, contracted such an admiration in the years of his childhood, and retained it faithfully through his life. Through the school and through the world, whithersoever his strange fortune led this erring, wayward, affectionate creature, Joseph Addison was always his head boy. Addison wrote his exercises. Addison did his best themes. He ran on Addison's messages; fagged for him and blacked his shoes: to be in Joe's company was Dick's greatest pleasure; and he took a sermon or a caning from his monitor with the most boundless reverence, acquiescence, and affection.

Steele found Addison a stately College Don at Oxford, and himself did not make much figure at this place. He wrote a comedy, which, by the advice of a friend, the humble fellow burned there; and some verses, which I dare say are as sublime as other gentlemen's compositions at that age; but being smitten with a sudden love for military glory, he threw up the cap and gown for the saddle and bridle, and rode privately in the Horse Guards, in the Duke of Ormond's troop—the second—and, probably, with the rest of the gentlemen of his troop, "all mounted on black horses with white feathers in their hats, and scar-

Some Prefatory Notes

let coats richly laced," marched by King William, in Hyde Park, in November 1699, and a great show of the nobility, besides twenty thousand people, and above a thousand coaches.

But Steele could hardly have seen any actual service. He who wrote about himself, his mother, his wife, his loves, his debts, his friends, and the wine he drank, would have told us of his battles if he had seen any. His old patron, Ormond, probably got him his cornetcy in the Guards, from which he was promoted to be a captain in Lucas's Fusiliers, getting his company through the patronage of Lord Cutts, whose secretary he was, and to whom he dedicated his work called the "Christian Hero." As for Dick, whilst writing this ardent devotional work, he was deep in debt, in drink, and in all the follies of the town; it is related that all the officers of Lucas's, and the gentlemen of the Guards, laughed at Dick. And in truth a theologian in liquor is not a respectable object, and a hermit, though he may be out at elbows, must not be in debt to the tailor. Steele says of himself that he was always sinning and repenting. He beat his breast and cried most piteously when he *did* repent; but as soon as crying had made him thirsty, he fell to sinning again. In that charming paper in the *Tatler*, in which he records his father's death, his mother's griefs, his own most solemn and tender emotions, he says he is interrupted by the arrival of a hamper of wine, "the same as is to be sold at Garraway's, next week"; upon the receipt of which he sends for three friends, and they fall to instantly, "drinking two bottles apiece with great benefit to themselves, and not separating till two o'clock in the morning."

His life was so. Jack the drawer was always interrupting it, bringing him a bottle from the "Rose," or inviting him over to a bout there with Sir Plume and Mr. Diver: and Dick wiped his eyes, which were whimpering over his papers, took down his laced hat, put on his sword and wig, kissed his wife and children, told them a lie about pressing business, and went off to the "Rose" to the jolly fellows.

While Mr. Addison was abroad, and after he came home in rather a dismal way to wait upon Providence in his shabby lodging in the Haymarket, young Captain Steele was cutting a much smarter figure than that of his classical friend of Charterhouse Cloister and Maudlin Walk. Cannot one fancy Joseph Addison's calm smile and cold grey eyes following Dick for an instant, as he struts down the Mall to dine with the Guard at Saint James's, before he turns, with his sober pace and threadbare suit, to walk back to his lodgings up the two pair of stairs?

Addison's hour of success now came, and he was able to help our friend the "Christian Hero" in such a way, that, if there had been any chance of keeping that poor tipsy champion upon his legs, his fortune was safe, and his competence assured. Steele procured the place of Commissioner of Stamps: he wrote so richly, so gracefully often, so kindly always, with such a pleasant wit and easy frankness, with such a gush of good spirits and good humour, that his early papers may be compared to Addison's own, and are to be read, by a male reader at least, with quite an equal pleasure.

After the *Tatler* in 1711, the famous *Spectator* made its appearance, and this was followed, at various intervals, by many periodicals under the same editor—the *Guardian* —the *Englishman*—the *Lover*, whose love was rather insipid—the *Reader*, of whom the public saw no more after his second appearance—the *Theatre*, under the pseudonym of Sir John Edgar, which Steele wrote while Governor of

Some Prefatory Notes

the Royal Company of Comedians, to which post, and to that of Surveyor of the Royal Stables at Hampton Court, and to the Commission of the Peace for Middlesex, and to the honour of knighthood, Steele had been preferred soon after the accession of George I.; whose cause honest Dick had nobly fought, through disgrace and danger, against the most formidable enemies, against traitors and bullies, against Bolingbroke and Swift in the last reign. With the arrival of the King, that splendid conspiracy broke up, and a golden opportunity came to Dick Steele, whose hand, alas, was too careless to grip it.

Steele married twice; and outlived his places, his schemes, his wife, his income, his health, and almost everything but his kind heart. That ceased to trouble him in 1729, when he died, worn out and almost forgotten by his contemporaries, in Wales, where he had the remnant of a property.

Posterity has been kinder to this amiable creature; all women especially are bound to be grateful to Steele, as he was the first of our writers who really seemed to admire and respect them. Addison laughs equally at women; but, with the gentleness and politeness of his nature, smiles at them and watches them, as if they were harmless, half-witted, amusing, pretty creatures, only made to be men's playthings. It was Steele who first began to pay a manly homage to their goodness and understanding, as well as to their tenderness and beauty. In his comedies the heroes do not rant and rave about the divine beauties of Gloriana or Statira, as the characters were made to do in the chivalry romances and the high-flown dramas just going out of vogue; but Steele admires women's virtue, acknowledges their sense, and adores their purity and beauty, with an ardour and strength which should win the good-will of all women to their hearty and respectful champion. It is this ardour, this respect, this manliness, which make his comedies so pleasant and their heroes such fine gentlemen. He paid the finest compliment to a woman that perhaps ever was offered. Of one woman, whom Congreve had also admired and celebrated, Steele says, that "to have loved her was a liberal education." "How often," he says, dedicating a volume to his wife, "how often has your tenderness removed pain from my sick head, how often anguish from my afflicted heart! If there are such beings as guardian angels, they are thus employed. I cannot believe one of them to be more good in inclination, or more charming in form, than my wife." His breast seems to warm and his eyes to kindle when he meets with a good and beautiful woman, and it is with his heart as well as with his hat that he salutes her. About children, and all that relates to home, he is not less tender, and more than once speaks in apology of what he calls his softness. He would have been nothing without that delightful weakness. It is that which gives his works their worth and his style its charm. It, like his life, is full of faults and careless blunders; and redeemed, like that, by his sweet and compassionate nature.

THE COVERLEY PAPERS

Illustrated by Gordon Ross

A NOTE UPON THE TEXT

IN this edition the text of THE COVERLEY PAPERS is reproduced substantially as the authors corrected it for printing in *The Spectator*.

To preserve the freshness of the original style, this text reproduces the harmony of the authors' special method of punctuation; and their way of sometimes getting emphasis by turning to account the use of capitals, which in their hands was not wholly conventional; and their charming if erratic italicizations; and the rows of single inverted commas, like lacy fret-work down the sides of some of the pages.

Steele and Addison deliberately refused to give their readers translations of the mottoes and Latin quotations which adorn the openings of the Papers. In this edition, translations are placed in a body at the back of the book, for the edification of those who want them.

Also, for the edification of the twentieth-century reader who is not thoroughly familiar with the topical references to eighteenth-century London, at the back of the book is placed a series of explanatory notes taken from the notes prepared for their editions by Percy and Calder "to give the reader an enjoyment of allusions to past manners and events". Included with these notes are the dates of the first printings of the various chapters, all of which first appeared in *The Spectator* in 1711 and 1712; and the identification of the authors of the various chapters, Addison having written twenty, Budgell two, and Steele eight.

THE AUTHOR'S PREFACE

*Non fumum ex fulgore, sed ex fumo dare lucem
Cogitat, ut speciosa dehinc miracula promat.*
                                                HORACE

I HAVE observed, that a Reader seldom peruses a Book with Pleasure, until he knows whether the Writer of it be a black or a fair Man, of a mild or cholerick Disposition, Married or a Bachelor, with other Particulars of the like Nature, that conduce very much to the right understanding of an Author. To gratify this Curiosity, which is so natural to a Reader, I design this Paper and my next as Prefatory Discourses to my following Writings, and shall give some Account in them of the several Persons that are engaged in this Work. As the chief Trouble of Compiling, Digesting, and Correcting will fall to my Share, I must do myself the Justice to open the Work with my own History.

I was born to a small Hereditary Estate, which according to the Tradition of the Village where it lies, was bounded by the same Hedges and Ditches in *William* the Conqueror's Time that it is at present, and has been delivered down from Father to Son whole and entire without the Loss or Acquisition of a single Field or Meadow, during the

Space of six hundred Years. There runs a Story in the Family, that my Mother dreamt that she had brought forth a Judge: Whether this might proceed from a Law-Suit which was then depending in the Family, or my Father's being a Justice of the Peace, I cannot determine; for I am not so vain as to think it presaged any Dignity that I should arrive at in my future Life, though that was the Interpretation which the Neighbourhood put upon it. The Gravity of my Behaviour at my very first Appearance in the World, seemed to favour my Mother's Dream: For, as she has often told me, I threw away my Rattle before I was two Months old, and would not make use of my Coral until they had taken away the Bells from it.

As for the rest of my Infancy, there being nothing in it remarkable, I shall pass it over in Silence. I find, that, during my Nonage, I had the Reputation of a very sullen Youth, but was always a Favourite of my Schoolmaster, who used to say, *that my Parts were solid, and would wear well.* I had not been long at the University, before I distinguished myself by a most profound Silence; for during the Space of eight Years, excepting in the publick Exercises of the College, I scarce uttered the Quantity of an hundred Words; and indeed do not remember that I ever spoke three Sentences together in my whole Life. Whilst I was in this learned Body, I applied myself with so much Diligence to my Studies, that there

The Author's Preface

are very few celebrated Books, either in the learned or the modern Tongues, which I am not acquainted with.

Upon the Death of my Father, I was resolved to travel into foreign Countries, and therefore left the University, with the Character of an odd unaccountable Fellow, that had a great deal of Learning, if I would but show it. An insatiable Thirst after Knowledge carried me into all the Countries of *Europe*, in which there was any thing new or strange to be seen; nay, to such a Degree was my Curiosity raised, that having read the Controversies of some great Men concerning the Antiquities of *Egypt*, I made a Voyage to *Grand Cairo*, on purpose to take the Measure of a Pyramid: And as soon as I had set myself right in that Particular, returned to my native Country with great Satisfaction.

I have passed my latter Years in this City, where I am frequently seen in most publick Places, though there are not above half a dozen of my select Friends that know me; of whom my next Paper shall give a more particular Account. There is no Place of general Resort, wherein I do not often make my Appearance; sometimes I am seen thrusting my Head into a Round of Politicians at *Will's*, and listning with great Attention to the Narratives that are made in those little circular Audiences. Sometimes I smoke a Pipe at *Child's*, and whilst I seem attentive to nothing but the *Postman*, overhear the Conversation of every Table in the Room. I appear on *Sunday* Nights at St. *James's* Coffee-house, and sometimes join the little Committee of Politicks in the Inner-Room, as one who comes there to hear and improve. My Face is likewise very well known at the *Grecian*, the *Cocoa-Tree*, and in the Theatres both of *Drury-Lane* and the *Hay-Market*. I have been taken for a Merchant upon the *Exchange* for above these ten Years, and sometimes pass for a *Jew* in the Assembly of Stock-Jobbers at *Jonathan's:* in short, where-ever I see a Cluster of People, I always mix with them, though I never open my Lips but in my own Club.

Thus I live in the World rather as a Spectator of Mankind, than as one of the Species; by which Means I have made myself a Speculative Statesman, Soldier, Merchant, and Artizan, without ever meddling with any practical Part in Life. I am very well versed in the Theory of a Husband or a Father, and can discern the Errors in the Œconomy, Business, and Diversion of others, better than those who are engaged in them; as Standers-by discover Blots, which are apt to escape those who are in the Game. I never espoused any Party with Violence, and am resolved to observe an exact Neutrality between the Whigs and Tories, unless I shall be forced to declare myself by the Hostilities of either side. In short, I have acted in all the Parts of my Life as a Looker-on, which is the Character I intend to preserve in this Paper.

The Author's Preface

There are three very material Points which I have not spoken to in this Paper; and which, for several important Reasons, I must keep to myself, at least for some Time: I mean, an Account of my Name, my Age, and my Lodgings. I must confess, I would gratify my Reader in any Thing that is reasonable; but as for these three Particulars, though I am sensible they might tend very much to the Embellishment of my Paper, I cannot yet come to a Resolution of communicating them to the Publick. They would indeed draw me out of that Obscurity which I have enjoyed for many Years, and expose me in publick Places to several Salutes and Civilities, which have been always very disagreeable to me; for the greatest Pain I can suffer, is the being talked to, and being ſtared at. It is for this Reason likewise, that I keep my Complexion and Dress as very great Secrets; though it is not impossible, but I may make Discoveries of both in the Progress of the Work I have undertaken.

After having been thus particular upon myself, I shall in To-morrow's Paper give an Account of those Gentlemen who are concerned with me in this Work; for, as I have before intimated, a Plan of it is laid and concerted (as all other Matters of Importance are) in a Club. However, as my Friends have engaged me to ſtand in the Front, those who have a mind to correspond with me, may direct their Letters to the SPECTATOR, at Mr. *Buckley's* in

Little-Britain. For I must further acquaint the Reader, that though our Club meets only on *Tuesdays* and *Thursdays*, we have appointed a Committee to sit every Night, for the inspection of all such Papers as may contribute to the Advancement of the Public Weal.

THE SPECTATOR.

London, Thursday, March 1, 1710-11.

SIR ROGER DE COVERLEY
BY THE SPECTATOR

Chapter I: Sir Roger and the Club

Ast alii sex
Et plures uno conclamant ore.
JUVENAL

THE FIRST of our Society is a Gentleman of *Worcestershire*, of ancient Descent, a Baronet, his Name Sir ROGER DE COVERLEY. His Great Grandfather was Inventor of that famous Country-Dance which is called after him. All who know that Shire are very well acquainted with the Parts and Merits of Sir ROGER. He is a Gentleman that is very singular in his Behaviour, but his Singularities proceed from his good Sense, and are Contradictions to the Manners of the World, only as he thinks the World is in the wrong. However, this Humour creates him no Enemies, for he does nothing with Sourness or Obstinacy; and his being unconfined to Modes and Forms, makes him but the readier and more capable to please and oblige all who know him. When he is in

Town, he lives in *Soho-Square*. It is said, he keeps himself a Bachelor by reason he was crossed in Love by a perverse beautiful Widow of the next County to him. Before this Disappointment, Sir ROGER was what you call a fine Gentleman, had often supped with my Lord *Rochester* and Sir *George Etherege*, fought a Duel upon his first coming to Town, and kicked Bully *Dawson* in a publick Coffee-house for calling him Youngster. But being ill used by the above-mentioned Widow, he was very serious for a Year and a half; and though, his Temper being naturally jovial, he at last got over it, he grew careless of himself, and never dressed afterwards. He continues to wear a Coat and Doublet of the same Cut that were in Fashion at the Time of his Repulse, which, in his merry Humours, he tells us, has been in and out twelve Times since he first wore it. He is now in his fifty-sixth Year, cheerful, gay, and hearty; keeps a good House both in Town and Country; a great Lover of Mankind; but there is such a mirthful Cast in his Behaviour, that he is rather beloved than esteemed. His Tenants grow rich, his Servants look satisfied, all the young Women profess Love to him, and the young Men are glad of his Company: When he comes into a House he calls the Servants by their Names, and talks all the Way up Stairs to a Visit. I must not omit, that Sir ROGER is a Justice of the *Quorum;* that he fills the Chair at a Quarter-Session with great Abilities, and three Months ago gained universal Applause by explaining a Passage in the Game-Act.

The Gentleman next in Esteem and Authority among us, is another Bachelor, who is a Member of the *Inner-Temple;* a Man of great Probity, Wit, and Understanding; but he has chosen his Place of Residence rather to obey the Direction of an old humoursom Father, than in pursuit of his own Inclinations. He was placed there to study the Laws of the Land, and is the most learned of any of the House in those of the Stage. *Aristotle* and *Longinus* are much better understood by him than *Littleton* or *Coke.* The Father sends up every Post Questions relating to Marriage-Articles, Leases, and Tenures, in the Neighbourhood; all which Questions he agrees with an Attorney to answer and take care of in the Lump. He is studying the Passions themselves, when he should be inquiring into the Debates among Men which arise from them. He knows the Argument of each of the Orations of *Demosthenes* and *Tully*, but not one Case in the Reports of our own Courts. No one ever took him for a Fool, but none, except his intimate Friends, know he has a great deal of Wit. This Turn makes him at once both disinterested and agreeable: As few of his Thoughts are drawn from Business, they are most of them fit for Conversation. His Taste of Books is a little too just for the Age he lives in; he has read all, but approves of very few. His Familiarity with the Customs, Manners, Actions, and Writings of the Ancients, makes him a very delicate Observer of what occurs to him in the present World. He is an excellent Critick, and the Time of the Play is his Hour of Business; exactly at five he passes through *New-Inn*, crosses through *Russell-Court*, and takes a turn at *Wills* till the Play begins; he has his Shoes rubbed and his Periwig powdered at the Barber's as you go into the *Rose*. It is for the Good of the Audience when he is at a Play, for the Actors have an Ambition to please him.

The Person of next Consideration, is Sir ANDREW FREEPORT, a Merchant of great Eminence in the City of *London*. A Person of indefatigable Industry, strong Reason, and great Experience. His Notions of Trade are noble and generous, and (as every rich Man has usually some sly Way of Jesting, which would make no great Figure were he not a rich Man) he calls the Sea the *British Common*. He is acquainted with Commerce in all its Parts, and will tell you that it is a stupid and barbarous Way to extend Dominion by Arms; for true Power is to be got by Arts and Industry. He will often argue, that if this Part of our Trade were well cultivated, we should gain from one Nation; and if another, from another. I have heard him prove, that Diligence makes more lasting Acquisitions than Valour, and that Sloth has ruined more Nations than the Sword. He abounds in several frugal Maxims, amongst which the greatest Favourite is, 'A Penny saved is a Penny got.' A gen-

Sir Roger and the Club

eral Trader of good Sense is pleasanter Company than a general Scholar! and Sir ANDREW having a natural unaffected Eloquence, the Perspicuity of his Discourse gives the same Pleasure that Wit would in another Man. He has made his Fortunes himself; and says that *England* may be richer than other Kingdoms, by as plain Methods as he himself is richer than other Men; though at the same time I can say this of him, that there is not a Point in the Compass but blows home a Ship in which he is an Owner.

Next to Sir ANDREW in the Club-Room sits Captain SENTREY, a Gentleman of great Courage, good Understanding, but invincible Modesty. He is one of those that deserve very well, but are very awkward at putting their Talents within the Observation of such as should take notice of them. He was some Years a Captain, and also behaved himself with great Gallantry in several Engagements and at several Sieges; but having a small Estate of his own, and being next Heir to Sir ROGER, he has quitted a Way of Life in which no Man can rise suitably to his Merit, who is not something of a Courtier as well as a Soldier. I have heard him often lament, that in a Profession where Merit is placed in so conspicuous a View, Impudence should get the better of Modesty. When he has talked to this Purpose I never heard him make a sour Expression, but frankly confess that he left the World, because he was not fit for it. A strict Honesty and an even regular Behaviour, are in themselves

Obstacles to him that must press through Crowds, who endeavour at the same End with himself, the Favour of a Commander. He will however in his way of Talk excuse Generals, for not disposing according to Men's Desert, or enquiring into it: For, says he, that great Man who has a mind to help me, has as many to break through to come at me, as I have to come at him: Therefore he will conclude, that the Man who would make a Figure, especially in a Military Way, must get over all false Modesty, and assist his Patron against the Importunity of other Pretenders, by a proper Assurance in his own Vindication. He says it is a civil Cowardise to be backward in asserting what you ought to expect, as it is a military Fear to be slow in attacking when it is your Duty. With this Candor does the Gentleman speak of himself and others. The same Frankness runs through all his Conversation. The military Part of his Life has furnished him with many Adventures, in the Relation of which he is very agreeable to the Company; for he is never overbearing, though accustomed to command Men in the utmost Degree below him; nor ever too obsequious from an Habit of obeying Men highly above him.

But that our Society may not appear to be a Set of Humourists unacquainted with the Gallantries and Pleasures of the Age, we have among us the gallant WILL HONEYCOMB, a Gentleman who according to his Years should be in the Decline of his Life, but having ever been very careful of his Person, and al-

ways had a very easy Fortune, Time has made but a very little Impression, either by Wrinkles on his Forehead, or Traces in his Brain. His Person is well turned, of a good Height. He is very ready at that sort of Discourse with which Men usually entertain Women. He has all his Life dressed very well, and remembers Habits as others do Men. He can smile when one speaks to him, and laughs easily. He knows the History of every Mode, and can inform you from which of the *French* king's Wenches our Wives and Daughters had this Manner of curling their Hair, that Way of placing their Hoods; whose Frailty was covered by such a sort of Petticoat, and whose Vanity to shew her Foot made that Part of the Dress so short in such a Year. In a word, all his Conversation and Knowledge have been in the female World: as other Men of his Age will take notice to you what such a Minister said upon such and such an Occasion, he will tell you when the Duke of *Monmouth* danced at Court, such a Woman was then smitten, another was taken with him at the Head of his Troop in the *Park*. In all these important Relations, he has ever about the same time received a kind Glance or a Blow of a Fan from some celebrated Beauty, Mother of the present Lord such-a-one. If you speak of a young Commoner that said a lively thing in the House, he starts up, 'He has good Blood in his Veins, *Tom Mira-*
'*bell*, the Rogue, cheated me in that Affair: that
' young Fellow's Mother used me more like a Dog
' than any Woman I ever made Advances to.' This

way of Talking of his very much enlivens the Conversation among us of a more sedate Turn; and I find there is not one of the Company, but myself, who rarely speak at all, but speaks of him as of that sort of Man who is usually called a well-bred fine Gentleman. To conclude his Character, where Women are not concerned, he is an honest worthy Man.

I cannot tell whether I am to account him whom I am next to speak of, as one of our Company; for he visits us but seldom, but when he does it adds to every Man else a new enjoyment of himself. He is a Clergyman, a very Philosophick Man, of general Learning, great Sanctity of Life, and the most exact good Breeding. He has the Misfortune to be of a very weak Constitution, and consequently cannot accept of such Cares and Business as Preferments in his Function would oblige him to: He is therefore among Divines what a Chamber-Counsellor is among Lawyers. The Probity of his Mind, and the Integrity of his Life, create him Followers, as being eloquent or loud advances others. He seldom introduces the Subject he speaks upon; but we are so far gone in Years, that he observes when he is among us, an Earnestness to have him fall on some divine Topick, which he always treats with much Authority, as one who has no Interests in this World, as one who is hastening to the Object of all his Wishes, and conceives Hope from his Decays and Infirmities. These are my ordinary Companions.

Chapter II: Coverley Hall

Hinc tibi Copia
Manabit ad plenum, benigno
Ruris honorum opulenta cornu.
HORACE

HAVING often received an Invitation from my Friend Sir ROGER DE COVERLEY to pass away a Month with him in the Country, I last Week accompanied him thither, and am settled with him for some Time at his Country-house, where I intend to form several of my ensuing Speculations. Sir ROGER, who is very well acquainted with my Humour, lets me rise and go to Bed when I please, dine at his own Table or in my Chamber as I think fit, sit still and say nothing without bidding me be merry. When the Gentlemen of the County come to see him, he only shows me at a distance: As I have been walking in his Fields I have observed them stealing a Sight of me over an Hedge, and have heard the Knight desiring them not to let me see them, for that I hated to be stared at.

I am the more at Ease in Sir ROGER's Family, because it consists of sober and staid Persons; for as the Knight is the best Master in the World, he seldom changes his Servants; and as he is beloved by all about

The Coverley Papers

him, his Servants never care for leaving him; by this means his Domesticks are all in Years, and grown old with their Master. You would take his Valet de Chambre for his Brother, his Butler is Greyheaded, his Groom is one of the gravest Men that I have ever seen, and his Coachman has the Looks of a Privy-Counsellor. You see the Goodness of the Master even in the old House-dog, and in a gray Pad that is kept in the Stable with great Care and Tenderness out of Regard to his past Services, though he has been useless for several Years.

I could not but observe with a great deal of Pleasure the Joy that appeared in the Countenances of these ancient Domesticks upon my Friend's Arrival at his Country-Seat. Some of them could not refrain from Tears at the Sight of their old Master; every one of them press'd forward to do something for him, and seemed discouraged if they were not employed. At the same time the good old Knight, with a Mixture of the Father and the Master of the Family, tempered the Inquiries after his own Affairs with several kind Questions relating to themselves. This Humanity and Good-nature engages every Body to him, so that when he is pleasant upon any of them, all his Family are in good Humour, and none so much as the Person whom he diverts himself with: On the contrary, if he coughs, or betrays any Infirmity of old Age, it is easy for a Stander-by to observe a secret Concern in the Looks of all his Servants.

Coverley Hall

My worthy Friend has put me under the particular Care of his Butler, who is a very prudent Man, and, as well as the rest of his Fellow-Servants, wonderfully desirous of pleasing me, because they have often heard their Master talk of me as of his particular Friend.

My chief Companion, when Sir Roger is diverting himself in the Woods or the Fields, is a very venerable Man who is ever with Sir Roger, and has lived at his House in the Nature of a Chaplain above thirty Years. This Gentleman is a Person of good Sense and some Learning, of a very regular Life and obliging Conversation: He heartily loves Sir Roger, and knows that he is very much in the old Knight's Esteem, so that he lives in the Family rather as a Relation than a Dependent.

I have observed in several of my Papers, that my Friend Sir Roger, amidst all his good Qualities, is something of an Humourist; and that his Virtues, as well as Imperfections, are as it were tinged by a certain Extravagance, which makes them particularly *his*, and distinguishes them from those of other Men. This Cast of Mind, as it is generally very innocent in itself, so it renders his Conversation highly agreeable, and more delightful than the same Degree of Sense and Virtue would appear in their common and ordinary Colours. As I was walking with him last Night, he asked me how I liked the good Man whom I have just now mentioned? and without staying for my

Answer told me, That he was afraid of being insulted with Latin and Greek at his own Table; for which Reason he desired a particular Friend of his then at the University to find him out a Clergyman rather of plain Sense than much Learning, of a good Aspect, a clear Voice, a sociable Temper; and, if possible, a Man that understood a little of Back-Gammon. My Friend, says Sir ROGER, found me out this Gentleman, who, besides the Endowments required of him, is, they tell me, a good Scholar, though he does not show it: I have given him the Parsonage of the Parish; and because I know his Value, have settled upon him a good Annuity for Life. If he outlives me, he shall find that he was higher in my Esteem than perhaps he thinks he is. He has now been with me thirty Years; and though he does not know I have taken notice of it, has never in all that time asked any thing of me for himself, though he is every Day soliciting me for something in Behalf of one or other of my Tenants his Parishioners. There has not been a Law-suit in the Parish since he has lived among them: if any Dispute arises, they apply themselves to him for the Decision; if they do not acquiesce in his Judgment, which I think never happened above once or twice at most, they appeal to me. At his first settling with me, I made him a Present of all the good Sermons which have been printed in *English*, and only begged of him that every *Sunday* he would pronounce one of them in the Pulpit. Accordingly he has digested them into such a Series, that

A very venerable man
of good sense and some learning

they follow one another naturally, and make a continued System of practical Divinity.

As Sir ROGER was going on in his Story, the Gentleman we were talking of came up to us; and upon the Knight's asking him who preached Tomorrow (for it was *Saturday* Night) told us, the Bishop of St. *Asaph* in the Morning, and Dr. *South* in the Afternoon. He then shewed us his List of Preachers for the whole Year, where I saw with a great deal of Pleasure Archbishop *Tillotson*, Bishop *Saunderson*, Dr. *Barrow*, Dr. *Calamy*, with several living Authors who have published Discourses of Practical Divinity. I no sooner saw this venerable Man in the Pulpit, but I very much approved of my Friend's insisting upon the Qualifications of a good Aspect and a clear Voice; for I was so charmed with the Gracefulness of his Figure and Delivery, as well as with the Discourses he pronounced, that I think I never passed any Time more to my Satisfaction. A Sermon repeated after this Manner, is like the Composition of a Poet in the Mouth of a graceful Actor.

I could heartily wish that more of our Country-Clergy would follow this Example; and instead of wasting their Spirits in laborious Compositions of their own, would endeavour after a handsom Elocution, and all those other Talents that are proper to enforce what has been penned by greater Masters. This would not only be more easy to themselves, but more edifying to the People.

Chapter III: The Coverley Household

Æsopo ingentem statuam posuere Attici,
Servumque collocârunt Æterna in Basi,
Patere honoris scirent ut Cunctis viam.

PHÆDRUS

THE Reception, manner of Attendance, undisturbed Freedom and Quiet, which I meet with here in the Country, has confirmed me in the Opinion I always had, that the general Corruption of Manners in Servants is owing to the Conduct of Masters. The Aspect of every one in the Family carries so much Satisfaction, that it appears he knows the happy Lot which has befàllen him in being a Member of it. There is one Particular which I have seldom seen but at Sir ROGER's; it is usual in all other places, that Servants fly from the Parts of the House through which their Master is passing: on the contrary, here they industriously place themselves in his way; and it is on both Sides, as it were, understood as a Visit, when the Servants appear without calling. This proceeds from the human and equal Temper of the Man of the House, who also perfectly well knows how to enjoy a great Estate, with such Oeconomy as ever to be much beforehand. This makes his own Mind untroubled, and consequently unapt to vent peevish Expressions, or give passionate or inconsistent Orders to those about him. Thus Respect and Love go together; and a certain Chearfulness in Performance of their Duty is the particular Distinction of the lower Part of this Family. When a Servant is called before his Master, he does not come with an Expectation to hear himself rated for some trivial Fault, threatened to be stripped or used with any other unbecoming Language, which mean Masters often give to worthy Servants; but it is often to know, what Road he took that he came so readily back according to Order; whether he passed by such a Ground, if the old Man who rents it is in good Health; or whether he gave Sir ROGER's Love to him, or the like.

A Man who preserves a Respect, founded on his Benevolence to his Dependents, lives rather like a Prince than a Master in his Family; his Orders are received as Favours, rather than Duties; and the Distinction of approaching him is Part of the Reward for executing what is commanded by him.

There is another Circumstance in which my Friend excels in his Management, which is the Manner of rewarding his Servants: He has ever been of Opinion, that giving his cast Clothes to be worn by Valets has a very ill Effect upon little Minds, and creates a silly Sense of Equality between the Parties, in Persons affected only with outward things. I have heard him often pleasant on this Occasion, and describe a young Gentleman abusing his Man in that

The Coverley Papers

Coat, which a Month or two before was the most pleasing Distinction he was conscious of in himself. He would turn his Discourse still more pleasantly upon the Ladies Bounties of this kind; and I have heard him say he knew a fine Woman, who distributed Rewards and Punishments in giving becoming or unbecoming Dresses to her Maids.

But my good Friend is above these little Instances of Good-will, in bestowing only Trifles on his Servants; a good Servant to him is sure of having it in his Choice very soon of being no Servant at all. As I before observed, he is so good an Husband, and knows so thoroughly that the Skill of the Purse is the Cardinal Virtue of this Life; I say, he knows so well that Frugality is the Support of Generosity, that he can often spare a large Fine when a Tenement falls, and give that Settlement to a good Servant who has a mind to go into the World, or make a Stranger pay the Fine to that Servant, for his more comfortable Maintenance, if he stays in his Service.

A Man of Honour and Generosity considers it would be miserable to himself to have no Will but that of another, though it were of the best Person breathing, and for that Reason goes on as fast as he is able to put his Servants into independent Livelihoods. The greatest Part of Sir ROGER's Estate is tenanted by Persons who have served himself or his Ancestors. It was to me extremely pleasant to observe the Visitants from several Parts to welcome his Arrival into

The Coverley Household

the Country; and all the Difference that I could take notice of between the late Servants who came to see him, and those who staid in the Family, was that these latter were looked upon as finer Gentlemen and better Courtiers.

This Manumission and placing them in a way of Livelihood, I look upon as only what is due to a good Servant, which Encouragement will make his Successor be as diligent, as humble, and as ready as he was. There is something wonderful in the Narrowness of those Minds, which can be pleased, and be barren of Bounty to those who please them.

One might, on this Occasion, recount the Sense that Great Persons in all Ages have had of the Merit of their Dependents, and the Heroic Services which Men have done their Masters in the Extremity of their Fortunes; and shewn to their undone Patrons, that Fortune was all the Difference between them; but as I design this my Speculation only as a gentle Admonition to thankless Masters, I shall not go out of the Occurrences of common Life, but assert it as a general Observation, that I never saw, but in Sir ROGER's Family, and one or two more, good Servants treated as they ought to be. Sir ROGER's Kindness extends to their Children's Children, and this very Morning he sent his Coachman's Grandson to Prentice. I shall conclude this Paper with an Account of a Picture in his Gallery, where there are many which will deserve my future Observation.

The Coverley Papers

At the very upper End of this handsom Structure I saw the Portraiture of two young Men standing in a River, the one Naked, the other in a Livery. The Person supported seemed half Dead, but still so much alive as to shew in his Face exquisite Joy and Love towards the other. I thought the fainting Figure resembled my Friend Sir ROGER; and looking at the Butler, who stood by me, for an Account of it, he informed me that the Person in the Livery was a Servant of Sir ROGER's, who stood on the Shore while his Master was swimming, and observing him taken with some sudden Illness, and sink under Water, jumped in and saved him. He told me Sir ROGER took off the Dress he was in as soon as he came home, and by a great Bounty at that time, followed by his Favour ever since, had made him Master of that pretty Seat which we saw at a distance as we came to this House. I remembered indeed Sir ROGER said there lived a very worthy Gentleman, to whom he was highly obliged, without mentioning any thing further. Upon my looking a little dissatisfyed at some part of the Picture, my Attendant informed me that it was against Sir ROGER's Will, and at the earnest Request of the Gentleman himself, that he was drawn in the Habit in which he had saved his Master.

Chapter IV: The Coverley Guest

Gratis anhelans, multa agendo nihil agens.
PHÆDRUS

AS I was Yesterday Morning walking with Sir ROGER before his House, a Country-Fellow brought him a huge Fish, which, he told him, Mr. *William Wimble* had caught that very Morning; and that he presented it, with his Service to him, and intended to come and dine with him. At the same time he delivered a Letter, which my Friend read to me as soon as the Messenger left him.
'*Sir* ROGER,

'I Desire you to accept of a Jack, which is the best
'I have caught this Season. I intend to come and ſtay
'with you a Week, and see how the Perch bite in the
'*Black River*. I observed with some Concern, the
'last time I saw you upon the Bowling-Green, that
'your Whip wanted a Lash to it; I will bring half a
'dozen with me that I twiſted last Week, which I
'hope will serve you all the Time you are in the
'Country. I have not been out of the Saddle for six
'Days last past, having been at *Eaton* with Sir *John*'s
'eldest Son. He takes to his Learning hugely. I am,
    '*Sir, Your Humble Servant,*
        '*W*ILL *W*IMBLE.'

The Coverley Papers

This extraordinary Letter, and Message that accompanied it, made me very curious to know the Character and Quality of the Gentleman who sent them; which I found to be as follows. *Will Wimble* is younger Brother to a Baronet, and descended of the ancient Family of the *Wimbles*. He is now between Forty and Fifty; but being bred to no Business and born to no Estate, he generally lives with his elder Brother as Superintendent of his Game. He hunts a Pack of Dogs better than any Man in the Country, and is very famous for finding out a Hare. He is extremely well versed in all the little Handicrafts of an idle Man: He makes a *May-fly* to a Miracle; and furnishes the whole Country with Angle-Rods. As he is a good-natured officious Fellow, and very much esteemed upon Account of his Family, he is a welcome Guest at every House, and keeps up a good Correspondence among all the Gentlemen about him. He carries a Tulip-Root in his Pocket from one to another, or exchanges a Puppy between a Couple of Friends that live perhaps in the opposite Sides of the Country. *Will* is a particular Favourite of all the young Heirs, whom he frequently obliges with a Net that he has weaved, or a Setting-dog that he has *made* himself. He now and then presents a Pair of Garters of his own knitting to their Mothers or Sisters; and raises a great deal of Mirth among them, by inquiring as often as he meets them *how they wear?* These Gentleman-like Manufactures and obliging little

Will Wimble

The Coverley Guest

humours make *Will* the Darling of the Country.

Sir ROGER was proceeding in the Character of him, when we saw him make up to us with two or three Hazle-twigs in his Hand that he had cut in Sir ROGER's Woods, as he came through them, in his Way to the House. I was very much pleased to observe on one Side the hearty and sincere Welcome with which Sir ROGER received him, and on the other, the secret Joy which his Guest discovered at Sight of the good old Knight. After the first Salutes were over, *Will* desired Sir ROGER to lend him one of his Servants to carry a Set of Shuttlecocks he had with him in a little Box to a Lady that lived about a Mile off, to whom it seems he had promised such a Present for above this half year. Sir ROGER's Back was no sooner turned but honest *Will* began to tell me of a large Cock-pheasant that he had sprung in one of the neighbouring Woods, with two or three other Adventures of the same Nature. Odd and uncommon Characters are the Game that I look for, and most delight in; for which Reason I was as much pleased with the Novelty of the Person that talked to me, as he could be for his Life with the springing of a Pheasant, and therefore listened to him with more than ordinary Attention.

In the midst of his Discourse the Bell rung to Dinner, where the Gentleman I have been speaking of had the pleasure of seeing the huge Jack, he had caught, served up for the first Dish in a most sumptuous manner. Upon our sitting down to it he gave us a long Account how he had hooked it, played with it, foiled it, and at length drew it out upon the Bank, with several other Particulars that lasted all the first Course. A Dish of Wildfowl that came afterwards furnished Conversation for the rest of the Dinner, which concluded with a late Invention of *Will's* for improving the Quail-pipe.

Upon withdrawing into my Room after Dinner, I was secretly touched with Compassion towards the honest Gentleman that had dined with us; and could not but consider with a great deal of Concern, how so good an Heart and such busy Hands were wholly employed in Trifles; that so much Humanity should be so little beneficial to others, and so much Industry so little advantageous to himself. The same Temper of Mind and Application to Affairs might have recommended him to the publick Esteem, and have raised his Fortune in another Station of Life. What Good to his Country or himself might not a Trader or a Merchant have done with such useful though ordinary Qualifications?

Will Wimble's is the Case of many a younger Brother of a great Family, who had rather see their Children starve like Gentlemen, than thrive in a Trade or Profession that is beneath their Quality. This Humour fills several Parts of *Europe* with Pride and Beggary. It is the Happiness of a Trading Nation, like ours, that the younger Sons, though unca-

The Coverley Guest

pable of any liberal Art or Profession, may be placed in such a way of Life, as may perhaps enable them to vie with the best of their Family: Accordingly we find several Citizens that were launched into the World with narrow Fortunes, rising by an honest Industry to greater Estates than those of their elder Brothers. It is not improbable but *Will* was formerly tried at Divinity, Law, or Physick; and that finding his Genius did not lie that Way, his Parents gave him up at length to his own Inventions. But certainly, however improper he might have been for Studies of a higher Nature, he was perfectly well turned for the Occupations of Trade and Commerce.

Chapter V: The Coverley Lineage

Abnormis sapiens.
HORACE

I WAS this Morning walking in the Gallery, when Sir ROGER entered at the End opposite to me, and advancing towards me, said he was glad to meet me among his Relations the DE COVERLEYS, and hoped I liked the Conversation of so much good Company, who were as silent as myself. I knew he alluded to the Pictures, and as he is a Gentleman who does not a little value himself upon his ancient Descent, I expected he would give me some Account of them. We are now arrived at the Upper-end of the Gallery, when the Knight faced towards one of the Pictures, and as we stood before it, he entered into the matter, after his blunt way of saying Things, as they occur to his Imagination, without regular Introduction, or Care to preserve the Appearance of Chain of Thought.

'It is,' said he, 'worth while to consider the
' Force of Dress; and how the Persons of one Age
' differ from those of another, merely by that only.
' One may observe also, that the general Fashion of
' one Age has been followed by one particular Set
' of People in another, and by them preserved from

The Coverley Lineage

'one Generation to another. Thus the vast jetting
'Coat and small Bonnet, which was the Habit in
'*Harry* the Seventh's Time, is kept on in the Yeo-
'men of the Guard; not without a good and politick
'View, because they look a Foot taller, and a Foot
'and an half broader: Besides that the Cap leaves
'the Face expanded, and consequently more terrible,
'and fitter to stand at the Entrance of Palaces.

'This Predecessor of ours, you see, is dressed after
'this manner, and his Cheeks would be no larger
'than mine, were he in a Hat as I am. He was the
'last Man that won a Prize in the Tilt-Yard (which
'is now a Common Street before *Whitehall*). You see
'the broken Lance that lies there by his right Foot;
'He shivered that Lance of his Adversary all to
'Pieces; and bearing himself, look you, Sir, in this
'manner, at the same time he came within the Tar-
'get of the Gentleman who rode against him, and
'taking him with incredible Force before him on
'the Pommel of his Saddle, he in that manner rid
'the Tournament over, with an Air that shewed he
'did it rather to perform the Rule of the Lists, than
'expose his Enemy; however, it appeared he knew
'how to make use of a Victory, and with a gentle
'Trot he marched up to a Gallery where their Mis-
'tress sat (for they were Rivals) and let him down
'with laudable Courtesy and pardonable Insolence.
'I don't know but it might be exactly where the
'Coffee-house is now.

The Coverley Papers

' You are to know this my Ancestor was not only
' of a military Genius, but fit also for the Arts of
' Peace, for he played on the Bass-Viol as well as any
' Gentlemen at Court; you see where his Viol hangs
' by his Basket-hilt Sword. The Action at the Tilt-
' yard you may be sure won the fair lady, who was a
' Maid of Honour, and the greatest Beauty of her
' Time; here she stands the next Picture. You see,
' Sir, my Great Great Great Grandmother has on
' the new-fashioned Petticoat, except that the Mod-
' ern is gathered at the Waste; my Grandmother ap-
' pears as if she stood in a large Drum, whereas the
' Ladies now walk as if they were in a Go-Cart. For
' all this Lady was bred at Court, she became an ex-
' cellent Country-Wife, she brought ten Children,
' and when I shew you the Library, you shall see in
' her own Hand, (allowing for the Difference of the
' Language) the best Receipt now in *England* both
' for an Hasty-pudding and a White-pot.

' If you please to walk back a little, because 'tis
' necessary to look at the three next Pictures at one
' View; these are three Sisters. She on the right
' Hand, who is so very beautiful, died a Maid: the
' next to her, still handsomer, had the same Fate,
' against her Will; this Homely Thing in the mid-
' dle had both their Portions added to her own, and
' was stolen by a neighbouring Gentleman, a Man of
' Stratagem and Resolution, for he poisoned three
' Mastiffs to come at her, and knocked down two

The Coverley Lineage

'Deer-stealers in carrying her off. Misfortunes hap-
'pen in all Families: The Theft of this Romp and
'so much Money, was no great matter to our Estate.
'But the next Heir that possessed it was this soft
'Gentleman, whom you see there: Observe the small
'Buttons, the little Boots, the Laces, the Slashes
'about his Clothes, and above all the Posture he is
'drawn in, (which to be sure was his own choos-
'ing;) you see he sits with one Hand on a Desk
'writing and looking as it were another way, like
'an easy Writer, or a Sonneteer: He was one of those
'that had too much Wit to know how to live in the
'World; he was a Man of no Justice, but great
'Good-Manners; he ruined every Body that had
'any thing to do with him, but never said a rude
'thing in his Life; the most indolent Person in the
'World, he would sign a Deed that passed away half
'his Estate with his Gloves on, but would not put
'on his Hat before a Lady if it were to save his
'Country. He is said to be the first that made Love
'by squeezing the Hand. He left the Estate with
'ten thousand Pounds Debt upon it: but however by
'all Hands I have been informed that he was every
'way the finest Gentleman in the World. That Debt
'lay heavy on our house for one Generation, but it
'was retrieved by a Gift from that honest Man you
'see there, a Citizen of our Name, but nothing at
'all akin to us. I know Sir ANDREW FREEPORT has
'said behind my Back, that this Man was descended

'from one of the ten Children of the Maid of
' Honour I shewed you above; but it was never made
' out. We winked at the thing indeed, because Money
' was wanting at that time.'

Here I saw my Friend a little embarrassed, and turned my Face to the next Portraiture.

Sir ROGER went on with his Account of the Gallery in the following manner. 'This Man' (pointing to him I looked at) ' I take to be the Honour of our
' House, Sir HUMPHREY DE COVERLEY; he was in
' his Dealings as punctual as a Tradesman, and as
' generous as a Gentleman. He would have thought
' himself as much undone by breaking his Word, as if
' it were to be followed by Bankruptcy. He served his
' Country as Knight of this Shire to his dying Day.
' He found it no easy matter to maintain an Integrity
' in his Words and Actions, even in things that re-
' garded the Offices which were incumbent upon him,
' in the Care of his own Affairs and Relations of Life,
' and therefore dreaded (though he had great Tal-
' ents) to go into Employments of State, where he
' must be exposed to the Snares of Ambition. Inno-
' cence of Life and great Ability were the Distin-
' guishing Parts of his Character; the latter, he had
' often observed, had led to the Destruction of the
' former, and used frequently to lament that Great
' and Good had not the same Signification. He was
' an excellent Husbandman, but had resolv'd not to
' exceed such a Degree of Wealth; all above it he be-

The Coverley Lineage

'stowed in secret Bounties many Years after the Sum
'he aimed at for his own Use was attained. Yet he
'did not slacken his Industry, but to a decent old Age
'spent the Life and Fortune which was superfluous
'to himself, in the Service of his Friends and Neigh-
'bours.'

Here we were called to Dinner, and Sir ROGER ended the Discourse of this Gentleman, by telling me, as we followed the Servant, that this his Ancestor was a brave Man, and narrowly escaped being killed in the Civil Wars; 'For,' said he, 'he was sent out of 'the Field upon a private Message, the Day before 'the Battle of *Worcester*.'

The Whim of narrowly escaping by having been within a Day of Danger, with other Matters above-mentioned, mixed with good Sense, left me at a loss whether I was more delighted with my Friend's Wisdom or Simplicity.

37

Chapter VI: The Coverley Ghost

Horror ubique animos, simul ipsa silentia terrent.
                                                    VIRGIL

AT a little distance from Sir ROGER's House, among the Ruins of an old Abbey, there is a long Walk of aged Elms; which are shot up so very high, that when one passes under them, the Rooks and Crows that rest upon the Tops of them seem to be Cawing in another Region. I am very much delighted with this sort of Noise, which I consider as a kind of natural Prayer to that Being who supplies the Wants of his whole Creation, and who, in the beautiful Language of the *Psalms*, feedeth the young Ravens that call upon him. I like this Retirement the better, because of an ill Report it lies under of being *haunted*; for which Reason (as I have been told in the Family) no living Creature ever walks in it besides the Chaplain. My good Friend the Butler desired me with a very grave Face not to venture myself in it after Sun-set, for that one of the Footmen had been almost frighted out of his Wits by a Spirit that appear'd to him in the Shape of a black Horse without an Head; to which he added, that about a Month ago one of the Maids coming home late that way with a Pail of Milk upon her Head, heard such a Rustling among the Bushes that she let it fall.

The Coverley Ghost

I was taking a Walk in this Place last Night between the Hours of Nine and Ten, and could not but fancy it one of the most proper Scenes in the World for a Ghost to appear in. The Ruins of the Abbey are scattered up and down on every Side, and half covered with Ivy and Elder-Bushes, the Harbours of several solitary Birds which seldom make their Appearance till the Dusk of the Evening. The Place was formerly a Churchyard, and has still several Marks in it of Graves and Burying-Places. There is such an Echo among the old Ruins and Vaults, that if you stamp but a little louder than ordinary, you hear the Sound repeated. At the same time the Walk of Elms, with the Croaking of the Ravens which from time to time are heard from the Tops of them, looks exceeding solemn and venerable. These Objects naturally raise Seriousness and Attention; and when Night heightens the Awfulness of the Place, and pours out her supernumerary Horrors upon every thing in it, I do not at all wonder that weak Minds fill it with Spectres and Apparitions.

Mr. *LOCKE*, in his Chapter of the Association of Ideas has very curious Remarks to shew how by the Prejudice of Education one Idea often introduces into the Mind a whole Set that bear no Resemblance to one another in the Nature of things. Among several Examples of this Kind, he produces the following Instance. *The Ideas of Goblins and Sprights have really no more to do with Darkness than Light: Yet let but a foolish Maid inculcate these often on the*

The Coverley Papers

Mind of a Child, and raise them there together, possibly he shall never be able to separate them again so long as he lives; but Darkness shall ever afterwards bring with it those frightful Ideas, and they shall be so joined that he can no more bear the one than the other.

As I was walking in this Solitude, where the Dusk of the Evening conspired with so many other Occasions of Terror, I observed a Cow grazing not far from me, which an Imagination that was apt to startle might easily have construed into a black Horse without an Head: And I dare say the poor Footman lost his Wits upon some such trivial Occasion.

My Friend Sir ROGER has often told me with a good deal of Mirth, that at his first coming to his Estate he found three Parts of his House altogether useless; that the best Room in it had the Reputation of being haunted, and by that means was locked up; that Noises had been heard in his long Gallery, so that he could not get a Servant to enter it after eight o'Clock at Night; that the Door of one of his Chambers was nailed up, because there went a Story in the Family that a Butler had formerly hang'd himself in it; and that his Mother, who lived to a great Age, had shut up half the Rooms in the House, in which either her Husband, a Son, or Daughter had died. The Knight seeing his Habitation reduced to so small a Compass, and himself in a manner shut out of his own House, upon the Death of his Mother ordered

The Coverley Ghost

all the Apartments to be flung open and *exorcised* by his Chaplain, who lay in every Room one after another, and by that means dissipated the Fears which had so long reigned in the Family.

I should not have been thus particular upon these ridiculous Horrors, did not I find them so very much prevail in all Parts of the Country. At the same time I think a Person who is thus terrify'd with the Imagination of Ghosts and Spectres much more reasonable than one who, contrary to the Report of all Historians sacred and profane, ancient and modern, and to the Traditions of all Nations, thinks the Appearance of Spirits fabulous and groundless: Could not I give myself up to this general Testimony of Mankind, I should to the Relations of particular Persons who are now living, and whom I cannot distrust in other Matters of Fact. I might here add, that not only the Historians, to whom we may join the Poets, but likewise the Philosophers of Antiquity have favoured this Opinion.

Chapter VII: The Coverley Sabbath

'Αθανάτους μὲν πρῶτα θεούς, νόμῳ ὡς διάκειται, Τιμᾶ.
                                                PYTHAGORAS

I AM always very well pleased with a Country *Sunday*, and think, if keeping holy the seventh Day were only a human Institution, it would be the best Method that could have been thought of for the polishing and civilizing of Mankind. It is certain the Country-People would soon degenerate into a kind of Savages and Barbarians, were there not such frequent Returns of a stated Time, in which the whole Village meet together with their best Faces, and in their cleanliest Habits to converse with one another upon indifferent Subjects, hear their Duties explained to them, and join together in Adoration of the Supreme Being. *Sunday* clears away the Rust of the whole Week, not only as it refreshes in their Minds the Notions of Religion, but as it puts both the Sexes upon appearing in their most agreeable Forms, and exerting all such Qualities as are apt to give them a Figure in the Eye of the Village. A Country Fellow distinguishes himself as much in the *Church-yard*, as a Citizen does upon the *Change*, the whole Parish-Politicks being generally discussed in that Place either after Sermon or before the Bell rings.

The Coverley Sabbath

My Friend Sir ROGER; being a good Churchman, has beautified the Inside of his Church with several Texts of his own choosing: He has likewise given a handsom Pulpit-Cloth, and railed in the Communion-Table at his own Expence. He has often told me, that at his coming to his Estate he found his Parishioners very irregular; and that in order to make them kneel and join in the Responses, he gave every one of them a Hassock and a Common-prayer Book: and at the same time employed an itinerant Singing Master, who goes about the Country for that purpose, to instruct them rightly in the Tunes of the Psalms; upon which they now very much value themselves, and indeed out-do most of the Country Churches that I have ever heard.

As Sir ROGER is Landlord to the whole Congregation, he keeps them in very good Order, and will suffer no body to sleep in it besides himself; for if by chance he has been surprised into a short Nap at Sermon, upon recovering out of it he stands up and looks about him, and if he sees any Body else nodding, either wakes them himself, or sends his Servants to them. Several other of the old Knight's Particularities break out upon these Occasions: Sometimes he will be lengthening out a Verse in the Singing-Psalms, half a Minute after the rest of the Congregation have done with it; sometimes, when he is pleased with the Matter of his Devotion, he pronounces *Amen* three or four times to the same Prayer; and sometimes stands up when every Body else is upon their Knees, to count the Congregation, or see if any of his Tenants are missing.

I was yesterday very much surprised to hear my old Friend, in the midst of the Service, calling out to one *John Matthews* to mind what he was about, and not disturb the Congregation. This *John Matthews* it seems is remarkable for being an idle Fellow, and at that time was kicking his Heels for his Diversion. This Authority of the Knight, though exerted in that odd manner which accompanies him in all Circumstances of Life, has a very good Effect upon the Parish, who are not polite enough to see any thing ridiculous in his Behaviour; besides that the general good Sense and Worthiness of his Character makes his Friends observe these little Singularities as Foils that rather set off than blemish his good Qualities.

As soon as the Sermon is finished, no body presumes to stir till Sir Roger is gone out of the Church. The Knight walks down from his Seat in the Chancel between a double Row of his Tenants, that stand bowing to him on each Side: and every now and then inquires how such an one's Wife, or Mother, or Son, or Father do, whom he does not see at Church; which is understood as a secret Reprimand to the Person that is absent.

The Chaplain has often told me, that upon a Catechising Day, when Sir Roger has been pleased with a Boy that answers well, he has ordered a Bible to be

The Coverley Sabbath

given him next Day for his Encouragement; and sometimes accompanies it with a Flitch of Bacon to his Mother. Sir ROGER has likewise added five Pounds a Year to the Clerk's Place; and that he may encourage the young Fellows to make themselves perfect in the Church-Service, has promised upon the Death of the present Incumbent, who is very old, to bestow it according to Merit.

The fair Understanding between Sir ROGER and his Chaplain, and their mutual Concurrence in doing Good, is the more remarkable, because the very next Village is famous for the Differences and Contentions that rise between the Parson and the 'Squire, who live in a perpetual State of War. The Parson is always preaching at the 'Squire, and the 'Squire to be revenged on the Parson never comes to Church. The 'Squire has made all his Tenants Atheists and Tithe-Stealers; while the Parson instructs them every *Sunday* in the Dignity of his Order, and insinuates to them in almost every Sermon, that he is a better Man than his Patron. In short, Matters are come to such an Extremity, that the 'Squire has not said his Prayers either in public or private this half Year; and that the Parson threatens him, if he does not mend his Manners, to pray for him in the Face of the whole Congregation.

Feuds of this Nature, though too frequent in the Country, are very fatal to the ordinary People; who are so used to be dazzled with Riches, that they pay

The Coverley Papers

as much Deference to the Understanding of a Man of an Estate, as of a Man of Learning; and are very hardly brought to regard any Truth, how important soever it may be, that is preached to them, when they know there are several Men of five hundred a Year who do not believe it.

Chapter VIII: Sir Roger in Love

Hærent infixi pectore vultus.
VIRGIL

IN my first Description of the Company in which I pass most of my Time, it may be remembered that I mentioned a great Affliction which my Friend Sir ROGER had met with in his Youth; which was no less than a Disappointment in Love. It happened this Evening, that we fell into a very pleasing Walk at a Distance from his House: As soon as we came into it, 'It is,' quoth the good old Man, looking round him with a Smile, 'very hard, that any Part
' of my Land should be settled upon one who has
' used me so ill as the perverse Widow did; and yet
' I am sure I could not see a Sprig of any Bough of
' this whole Walk of Trees, but I should reflect upon
' her and her Severity. She has certainly the finest
' Hand of any Woman in the World. You are to know
' this was the Place wherein I used to muse upon her;
' and by that Custom I can never come into it, but the
' same tender Sentiments revive in my Mind, as if I
' had actually walked with that beautiful Creature
' under these Shades. I have been Fool enough to
' carve her Name on the Bark of several of these
' Trees; so unhappy is the Condition of Men in Love,

47

'to attempt the removing of their Passions by the
'Methods which serve only to imprint it deeper. She
'has certainly the finest Hand of any Woman in the
'World.'

Here followed a profound Silence; and I was not displeased to observe my Friend falling so naturally into a Discourse, which I had ever before taken notice he industriously avoided. After a very long Pause he entered upon an Account of this great Circumstance in his Life, with an Air which I thought raised my Idea of him above what I had ever had before; and gave me the Picture of that cheerful Mind of his, before it received that Stroke which has ever since affected his Words and Actions. But he went on as follows.

'I came to my Estate in my Twenty second Year,
'and resolved to follow the Steps of the most worthy
'of my Ancestors who have inhabited this Spot of
'Earth before me, in all the Methods of Hospitality
'and good Neighbourhood, for the sake of my Fame;
'and in Country Sports and Recreations, for the sake
'of my Health. In my Twenty third Year I was
'obliged to serve as Sheriff of the County; and in my
'Servants, Officers and whole Equipage, indulged
'the Pleasure of a young Man (who did not think ill
'of his own Person) in taking that public Occasion
'of shewing my Figure and Behaviour to Advantage.
'You may easily imagine to yourself what Appear-
'ance I made, who am pretty tall, rid well, and was

*I have been
fool enough to carve her name*

Sir Roger in Love

'very well dressed, at the Head of a whole County,
' with Musick before me, a Feather in my Hat, and
' my Horse well bitted. I can assure you I was not a
' little pleased with the kind Looks and Glances I had
' from all the Balconies and Windows as I rode to the
' Hall where the Assizes were held. But when I came
' there, a beautiful Creature in a Widow's Habit sat
' in Court, to hear the Event of a Cause concerning
' her Dower. This commanding Creature (who was
' born for Destruction of all who behold her) put on
' such a Resignation in her Countenance, and bore
' the Whispers of all around the Court, with such a
' pretty Uneasiness, I warrant you, and then recov-
' ered herself from one Eye to another, 'till she was
' perfectly confused by meeting something so wistful
' in all she encountered, that at last, with a Murrain
' to her, she cast her bewitching Eye upon me. I no
' sooner met it, but I bowed like a great surprised
' Booby; and knowing her Cause to be the first which
' came on, I cried, like a captivated Calf as I was,
' Make way for the Defendant's Witnesses. This sud-
' den Partiality made all the County immediately see
' the Sheriff also was become a Slave to the fine
' Widow. During the Time her Cause was upon Trial,
' she behaved herself, I warrant you, with such a deep
' Attention to her Business, took Opportunities to
' have little Billets handed to her Counsel, then would
' be in such a pretty Confusion, occasioned, you must
' know, by acting before so much Company, that not

'only I but the whole Court was prejudiced in her
'Favour; and all that the next Heir to her Husband
'had to urge, was thought so groundless and friv-
'olous, that when it came to her Counsel to reply,
'there was not half so much said as every one besides
'in the Court thought he could have urged to her
'Advantage. You must understand, Sir, this perverse
'Woman is one of those unaccountable Creatures,
'that secretly rejoice in the Admiration of Men,
'but indulge themselves in no farther Consequences.
'Hence it is that she has ever had a Train of Ad-
'mirers, and she removes from her Slaves in Town
'to those in the Country, according to the Seasons of
'the Year. She is a reading Lady, and far gone in the
'Pleasures of Friendship: She is always accompanied
'by a Confident, who is Witness to her daily Prot-
'estations against our Sex, and consequently a Bar
'to her first Steps towards Love, upon the Strength
'of her own Maxims and Declarations.

'However, I must needs say this accomplished
'Mistress of mine has distinguished me above the
'rest, and has been known to declare Sir ROGER
'DE COVERLEY was the tamest and most humane
'of all the Brutes in the Country. I was told she said
'so by one who thought he rallied me; but upon the
'Strength of this slender Encouragement of being
'thought least detestable I made new Liveries, new-
'paired my Coach-Horses, sent them all to Town to
'be bitted, and taught to throw their Legs well, and

Sir Roger in Love

'move all together, before I pretended to cross the
' Country and wait upon her. As soon as I thought
' my Retinue suitable to the Character of my Fortune
' and Youth, I set out from hence to make my Ad-
' dresses. The particular Skill of this Lady has ever
' been to inflame your Wishes, and yet command Re-
' spect. To make her Mistress of this Art, she has a
' greater Share of Knowledge, Wit, and good Sense,
' than is usual even among Men of Merit. Then she
' is beautiful beyond the Race of Women. If you
' won't let her go on with a certain Artifice with her
' Eyes, and the Skill of Beauty, she will arm herself
' with her real Charms, and strike you with Admira-
' tion. It is certain that if you were to behold the
' whole Woman, there is that Dignity in her Aspect,
' that Composure in her Motion, that Complacency
' in her Manner, that if her Form makes you hope,
' her Merit makes you fear. But then again, she is
' such a desperate Scholar, that no Country-Gentle-
' man can approach her without being a Jest. As I
' was going to tell you, when I came to her House I
' was admitted to her Presence with great Civility;
' at the same time she placed herself to be first seen
' by me in such an Attitude, as I think you call the
' Posture of a Picture, that she discovered new
' Charms, and I at last came towards her with such
' an Awe as made me speechless. This she no sooner
' observed but she made her Advantage of it, and be-
' gan to Discourse to me concerning Love and Hon-

' our, as they both are followed by Pretenders, and
' the real Votaries to them. When she discussed these
' Points in a Discourse, which I verily believe was as
' learned as the best Philosopher in *Europe* could pos-
' sibly make, she asked me whether she was so happy
' as to fall in with my Sentiments on these important
' Particulars. Her Confident sat by her, and upon
' my being in the last Confusion and Silence, this
' malicious Aid of hers turning to her says, I am very
' glad to observe Sir ROGER pauses upon this Subject,
' and seems resolved to deliver all his Sentiments
' upon the Matter when he pleases to speak. They
' both kept their Countenances, and after I had sat
' half an Hour meditating how to behave before such
' profound Casuists, I rose up and took my Leave.
' Chance has since that time thrown me very often
' in her way, and she as often has directed a Discourse
' to me which I do not understand. This Barbarity
' has kept me ever at a distance from the most beauti-
' ful Object my Eyes ever beheld. It is thus also she
' deals with all Mankind, and you must make Love
' to her, as you would conquer the Sphinx, by posing
' her. But were she like other Women, and that there
' were any talking to her, how constant must the
' Pleasure of that Man be, who could converse with
' a Creature———But, after all, you may be sure her
' Heart is fixed on some one or other; and yet I have
' been credibly informed; but who can believe half
' that is said! After she had done speaking to me, she

Sir Roger in Love

'put her Hand to her Bosom and adjusted her Tucker.
'Then she cast her Eyes a little down, upon my be-
'holding her too earnestly. They say she sings excel-
'lently: her Voice in her ordinary Speech has some-
'thing in it inexpressibly sweet. You must know I
'dined with her at a publick Table the Day after I
'first saw her, and she helped me to some Tansy in
'the Eye of all the Gentlemen in the Country: She
'has certainly the finest Hand of any Woman in the
'World. I can assure you, Sir, were you to behold her,
'you would be in the same Condition; for as her
'Speech is Musick, her Form is Angelick. But I find
'I grow irregular while I am talking of her; but in-
'deed it would be Stupidity to be unconcerned at
'such Perfection. Oh the excellent Creature! she is
'as inimitable to all Women, as she is inaccessible to
'all Men.'

I found my Friend begin to rave, and insensibly led him towards the House, that we might be joined by some other Company; and am convinced that the Widow is the secret Cause of all that Inconsistency which appears in some Parts of my Friend's Discourse; though he has so much Command of himself as not directly to mention her, yet according to that of *Martial* which one knows not how to render into *English*, *Dum tacet hanc loquitur*. I shall end this Paper with that whole Epigram, which represents with much Humour my honest Friend's Condition.

The Coverley Papers

Quicquid agit Rufus, nihil est, nisi Nævia Rufo,
Si gaudet, si flet, si tacet, hanc loquitur:
Cœnat, propinat, poscit, negat, annuit, una est
Nævia; Si non sit Nævia, mutus erit.
Scriberet hesternâ Patri cùm Luce Salutem,
Nævia lux, inquit, Nævia numen, ave.

Let *Rufus* weep, rejoice, stand, sit, or walk,
Still he can nothing but of *Nævia* talk;
Let him eat, drink, ask Questions, or dispute,
Still he must speak of *Nævia*, or be mute,
He writ to his Father, ending with this Line,
I am, my lovely *Nævia*, ever thine.

Chapter IX: The Coverley Oeconomy

Paupertatis pudor & fuga.
HORACE

OECONOMY in our Affairs has the same Effect upon our Fortunes which Good-breeding has upon our Conversations. There is a pretending Behaviour in both Cases, which, instead of making Men esteemed, renders them both miserable and contemptible. We had Yesterday at Sir ROGER's a Set of Country Gentlemen who dined with him: and after Dinner the Glass was taken, by those who pleased, pretty plentifully. Among others I observed a Person of a tolerable good Aspect, who seemed to be more greedy of Liquor than any of the Company, and yet, methought, he did not taste it with Delight. As he grew warm, he was suspicious of every thing that was said; and as he advanced towards being fuddled, his Humour grew worse. At the same time his Bitterness seemed to be rather an inward Dissatisfaction in his own Mind, than any Dislike he had taken to the Company. Upon hearing his Name, I knew him to be a Gentleman of a considerable Fortune in this County, but greatly in Debt. What gives the unhappy Man this Peevishness of Spirit, is, that his Estate is dipped, and is eating out with Usury; and yet he has not the Heart to sell any Part of it. His proud Stomach, at the Cost of restless Nights, constant Inquietudes, Danger of Affronts, and a thousand nameless Inconveniences, preserves this Canker in his Fortune, rather than it shall be said he is a Man of fewer Hundreds a Year than he has been commonly reputed. Thus he endures the Torment of Poverty, to avoid the Name of being less rich. If you go to his House you see great Plenty; but served in a Manner that shows it is all unnatural, and that the Master's Mind is not at Home. There is a certain Waste and Carelessness in the Air of every thing, and the whole appears but a covered Indigence, a magnificent Poverty. That Neatness and Chearfulness which attends the Table of him who lives within Compass, is wanting, and exchanged for a Libertine Way of Service in all about him.

This Gentleman's Conduct, though a very common way of Management, is as ridiculous as that Officer's would be, who had but few Men under his Command, and should take the Charge of an Extent of Country rather than of a small Pass. To pay for, personate, and keep in a Man's Hands, a greater Estate than he really has, is of all others the most unpardonable Vanity, and must in the End reduce the Man who is guilty of it to Dishonour. Yet if we look round us in any County of *Great Britain*, we shall see many in this fatal Error; if that may be called by so soft a Name, which proceeds from a false Shame of

The Coverley Oeconomy

appearing what they really are, when the contrary Behaviour would in a short time advance them to the Condition which they pretend to.

Laertes has fifteen hundred Pounds a Year; which is mortgaged for six thousand Pounds; but it is impossible to convince him that if he sold as much as would pay off that Debt, he would save four Shillings in the Pound, which he gives for the Vanity of being the reputed Master of it. Yet if *Laertes* did this, he would perhaps be easier in his own Fortune; but then *Irus*, a Fellow of Yesterday, who has but twelve hundred a Year, would be his Equal. Rather than this shall be, *Laertes* goes on to bring well-born Beggars into the World, and every Twelvemonth charges his Estate with at least one Year's Rent more by the Birth of a Child.

Laertes and *Irus* are Neighbours, whose Way of living are an Abomination each to the other. *Irus* is moved by the Fear of Poverty, and *Laertes* by the Shame of it. Though the Motive of Action is of so near Affinity in both, and may be resolved into this, " That to each of them Poverty is the greatest of all " Evils," yet are their Manners very widely different. Shame of Poverty makes *Laertes* lanch into unnecessary Equipage, vain Expence, and lavish Entertainments; Fear of Poverty makes *Irus* allow himself only plain Necessaries, appear without a Servant, sell his own Corn, attend his Labourers, and be himself a Labourer. Shame of Poverty makes *Laertes* go every Day a Step nearer to it, and Fear of Poverty stirs up *Irus* to make every Day some further Progress from it.

These different Motives produce the Excesses which Men are guilty of in the Negligence of and Provision for themselves. Usury, Stock-jobbing, Extortion and Oppression, have their Seed in the Dread of Want; and Vanity, Riot and Prodigality, from the Shame of it: But both these Excesses are infinitely below the Pursuit of a reasonable Creature. After we have taken care to command so much as is necessary for maintaining ourselves in the Order of Men suitable to our Character, the Care of Superfluities is a Vice no less extravagant, than the Neglect of Necessaries would have been before.

It would methinks be no ill Maxim of Life, if according to that Ancestor of Sir ROGER, whom I lately mentioned, every Man would point to himself what Sum he would resolve not to exceed. He might by this means cheat himself into a Tranquillity on this Side of that Expectation, or convert what he should get above it to nobler Uses than his own Pleasures or Necessities.

It is possible that the Tranquillity I now enjoy at Sir ROGER's may have created in me this way of thinking, which is so abstracted from the common Relish of the World: But as I am now in a pleasing Arbour surrounded with a beautiful Landskip, I find no Inclination so strong as to continue in these Man-

The Coverley Oeconomy

sions, so remote from the ostentatious Scenes of Life; and am at this present Writing Philosopher enough to conclude with Mr. *Cowley*,

> *If e'er Ambition did my Fancy cheat,*
> *With any Wish so mean as to be Great;*
> *Continue, Heaven, still from me to remove*
> *The humble Blessings of that Life I love!*

Chapter X: The Coverley Hunt

Ut sit Mens sana in corpore sano.
JUVENAL

HAD not Exercise been absolutely necessary for our Well-being, Nature would not have made the Body so proper for it, by giving such an Activity to the Limbs, and such a Pliancy to every Part as necessarily produce those Compressions, Extensions, Contortions, Dilatations, and all other kinds of Motions that are necessary for the preservation of such a System of Tubes and Glands as has been before mentioned. And that we might not want Inducements to engage us in such an Exercise of the Body as is proper for its Welfare, it is so ordered that nothing valuable can be procured without it. Not to mention Riches and Honour, even Food and Raiment are not to be come at without the Toil of the Hands and Sweat of the Brows. Providence furnishes Materials, but expects that we should work them up ourselves. The Earth must be laboured before it gives its Increase, and when it is forced into its several Products, how many Hands must they pass through before they are fit for Use? Manufactures, Trade, and Agriculture, naturally employ more than nineteen Parts of the Species in twenty; and as for those who are not

The Coverley Hunt

obliged to labour, by the Condition in which they are born, they are more miserable than the rest of Mankind, unless they indulge themselves in that voluntary Labour which goes by the Name of Exercise.

My Friend Sir ROGER has been an indefatigable Man in Business of this kind, and has hung several Parts of his House with the Trophies of his former Labours. The Walls of his great Hall are covered with the Horns of several kinds of Deer that he has killed in the Chace, which he thinks the most valuable Furniture of his House, as they afford him frequent Topicks of Discourse, and show that he has not been idle. At the lower End of the Hall is a large Otter's Skin stuffed with Hay, which his Mother ordered to be hung up in that manner, and the Knight looks upon with great Satisfaction, because it seems he was but nine Years old when his Dog killed him. A little Room adjoining to the Hall is a kind of Arsenal filled with Guns of several Sizes and Inventions, with which the Knight has made great Havock in the Woods, and destroyed many thousands of Pheasants, Partridges and Woodcocks. His Stable Doors are patched with Noses that belonged to Foxes of the Knight's own hunting down. Sir ROGER showed me one of them that for Distinction sake has a Brass Nail struck through it, which cost him about fifteen Hours riding, carried him through half a Dozen Counties, killed him a Brace of Geldings, and lost above half his Dogs. This the Knight looks upon as one of the greatest Exploits of his Life. The perverse Widow, whom I have given some Account of, was the Death of several Foxes; for Sir ROGER has told me that in the Course of his Amours he patched the Western Door of his Stable. Whenever the Widow was cruel, the Foxes were sure to pay for it. In Proportion as his Passion for the Widow abated and old Age came on, he left off Fox-hunting; but a Hare is not yet safe that sits within ten Miles of his House.

After what has been said, I need not inform my Readers, that Sir ROGER, with whose Character I hope they are at present pretty well acquainted, has in his Youth gone through the whole Course of those rural Diversions which the Country abounds in; and which seems to be extremely well suited to that laborious Industry a Man may observe here in a far greater Degree than in Towns and Cities. I have before hinted at some of my Friend's Exploits: He has in his youthful Days taken forty Coveys of Partridges in a Season; and tired many a Salmon with a Line consisting but of a single Hair. The constant Thanks and good Wishes of the Neighbourhood always attended him, on account of his remarkable Enmity towards Foxes; having destroyed more of those Vermin in one Year, than it was thought the whole Country could have produced. Indeed the Knight does not scruple to own among his most intimate Friends, that in order to establish his Reputation this Way, he has secretly sent for great Numbers of them out of other Counties,

The Coverley Hunt

which he used to turn loose about the Country by Night, that he might the better signalize himself in their Destruction the next Day. His Hunting-Horses were the finest and best managed in all these Parts: His Tenants are still full of the Praises of a gray Stone-horse that unhappily staked himself several Years since, and was buried with great Solemnity in the Orchard.

Sir ROGER, being at present too old for Fox-hunting, to keep himself in Action, has disposed of his Beagles and got a Pack of *Stop-hounds*. What these want in Speed, he endeavours to make amends for by the Deepness of their Mouths and the Variety of their Notes, which are suited in such manner to each other, that the whole Cry makes up a complete Consort. He is so nice in this Particular, that a Gentleman having made him a Present of a very fine Hound the other Day, the Knight returned it by the Servant with a great many Expressions of Civility; but desired him to tell his Master, that the Dog he had sent was indeed a most excellent *Bass*, but that at present he only wanted a *Counter-Tenor*. Could I believe my Friend had ever read Shakespeare, I should certainly conclude he had taken the Hint from *Theseus* in *the Midsummer Night's Dream*.

My Hounds are bred out of the Spartan *Kind,*
So flu'd, so sanded; and their Heads are hung
With Ears that sweep away the Morning Dew.

The Coverley Papers

Crook-kneed and dew-lap'd like Thessalian *Bulls.*
Slow in Pursuit, but match'd in Mouths like Bells,
Each under each: A Cry more tuneable
Was never hollowed to, nor chear'd with Horn.

Sir ROGER is so keen at this Sport, that he has been out almost every Day since I came down; and upon the Chaplain's offering to lend me his easy Pad, I was prevailed on Yesterday Morning to make one of the Company. I was extremely pleased, as we rid along, to observe the general Benevolence of all the Neighbourhood towards my Friend. The Farmers Sons thought themselves happy if they could open a Gate for the good old Knight as he passed by; which he generally requited with a Nod or a Smile, and a kind Inquiry after their Fathers and Uncles.

After we had rid about a Mile from Home, we came upon a large Heath, and the Sportsmen began to beat. They had done so for some time, when, as I was at a little Distance from the rest of the Company, I saw a Hare pop out from a small Furze-brake almost under my Horse's Feet. I marked the Way she took, which I endeavoured to make the Company sensible of by extending my Arm; but to no purpose, 'till Sir ROGER, who knows that none of my extraordinary Motions are insignificant, rode up to me and asked me *if Puss was gone that Way?* Upon my answering *Yes*, he immediately called in the Dogs, and put them upon the Scent. As they were going off,

Cheering the Hounds

The Coverley Hunt

I heard one of the Country-Fellows muttering to his Companion, *That 'twas a Wonder they had not lost all their Sport, for want of the silent Gentleman's crying Stole Away.*

This, with my Aversion to leaping Hedges, made me withdraw to a rising Ground, from whence I could have the Pleasure of the whole Chace, without the fine Fatigue of keeping in with the Hounds. The Hare immediately threw them above a Mile behind her; but I was pleased to find, that instead of running straight forwards, or in Hunter's Language, *Flying the Country*, as I was afraid she might have done, she wheeled about, and described a sort of Circle round the Hill where I had taken my Station, in such Manner as gave me a very distinct View of the Sport. I could see her first pass by, and the Dogs sometime afterwards while unravelling the whole Track she had made, and following her through all her Doubles. I was at the same time delighted in observing that Deference which the rest of the Pack paid to each particular Hound, according to the Character he had acquired amongst them: If they were at a Fault, and an old Hound of Reputation opened but once, he was immediately followed by the whole Cry; while a raw Dog, or one who was a noted *Liar*, might have yelped his Heart out, without being taken notice of.

The Hare now, after having squatted two or three times, and been put up again as often, came still nearer to the Place where she was at first started.

The Dogs pursued her, and these were followed by the jolly Knight, who rode upon a white Gelding, encompassed by his Tenants and Servants, and chearing his Hounds with all the Gaiety of Five and Twenty. One of the Sportsmen rode up to me, and told me, that he was sure the Chace was almost at an end, because the old Dogs, which had hitherto lain behind, now headed the Pack. The Fellow was in the right. Our Hare took a large Field just under us followed by the full Cry *in View*. I must confess the Brightness of the Weather, the Chearfulness of every thing around me, the *Chiding* of the Hounds, which was returned upon us in a double Echo from two neighbouring Hills, with the Hollowing of the Sportsmen, and the Sounding of the Horn, lifted my Spirits into a most lively Pleasure, which I freely indulged because I was sure it was *innocent*. If I was under any Concern, it was on the account of the poor Hare, that was now quite spent, and almost within the reach of her Enemies; when the Huntsman getting forward threw down his Pole before the Dogs. They were now within eight Yards of that Game which they had been pursuing for almost as many Hours; yet on the signal beforementioned they all made a sudden Stand, and though they continued opening as much as before, durst not once attempt to pass beyond the Pole. At the same time Sir ROGER rode forward, and alighting, took up the Hare in his Arms; which he soon delivered up to one of his Servants with an Order, if she could be

The Coverley Hunt

kept alive, to let her go in his great Orchard; where it seems he has several of these Prisoners of War, who live together in a very comfortable Captivity. I was highly pleased to see the Discipline of the Pack, and the Good-nature of the Knight, who could not find in his Heart to murder a Creature that had given him so much Diversion.

For my own part I intend to hunt twice a Week during my Stay with Sir ROGER; and shall prescribe the moderate Use of this Exercise to all my Country Friends, as the best kind of Physick for mending a bad Constitution, and preserving a good one.

I cannot do this better, than in the following Lines out of Mr. *Dryden*.

The first Physicians by Debauch were made;
Excess began, and Sloth sustains the Trade.
By Chace our long-lived Fathers earned their Food;
Toil strung the Nerves, and purify'd the Blood;
But we their Sons, a pamper'd Race of Men,
Are dwindled down to threescore Years and ten.
Better to hunt in Fields for Health unbought,
Than see the Doctor for a nauseous Draught.
The Wise for Cure on Exercise depend:
God never made his Work for Man to mend.

Chapter XI: The Coverley Witch

Ipsi sibi somnia fingunt.
VIRGIL

THERE are some Opinions in which a Man should stand Neuter, without engaging his Assent to one side or the other. Such a hovering Faith as this, which refuses to settle upon any Determination, is absolutely necessary in a Mind that is careful to avoid Errors and Prepossessions. When the Arguments press equally on both sides in Matters that are indifferent to us, the safest Method is to give up ourselves to neither.

It is with this Temper of Mind that I consider the Subject of Witchcraft. When I hear the Relations that are made from all Parts of the World, not only from *Norway* and *Lapland*, from the *East* and *West-Indies*, but from every particular Nation in *Europe*, I cannot forbear thinking that there is such an Intercourse and Commerce with Evil Spirits, as that which we express by the Name of Witchcraft. But when I consider that the ignorant and credulous Parts of the World abound most in these Relations, and that the Persons among us, who are supposed to engage in such an infernal Commerce, are People of a weak Understanding and crazed Imagination, and at the

The Coverley Witch

same time reflect upon the many Impostures and Delusions of this Nature that have been detected in all Ages, I endeavour to suspend my Belief till I hear more certain Accounts than any which have yet come to my Knowledge. In short, when I consider the Question, whether there are such Persons in the World as those we call Witches, my Mind is divided between the two opposite Opinions; or rather (to speak my Thoughts freely) I believe in general that there is, and has been such a thing as Witchcraft; but at the same time can give no Credit to any particular Instance of it.

I am engaged in this Speculation, by some Occurrences that I met with Yesterday, which I shall give my Reader an Account of at large. As I was walking with my Friend Sir ROGER by the side of one of his Woods, an old Woman applied herself to me for my Charity. Her Dress and Figure put me in mind of the following Description in *Otway*.

In a close Lane as I pursued my Journey,
I spy'd a wrinkled Hag, *with Age grown double,*
Picking dry Sticks, and mumbling to herself.
Her Eyes with scalding Rheum were gall'd and red;
Cold Palsy shook her Head; her Hands seem'd
   wither'd;
And on her crooked Shoulders had she wrapp'd
The tatter'd Remnants of an old striped Hanging,
Which served to keep her Carcass from the Cold:

So there was nothing of a Piece about her.
Her lower Weeds were all o'er coarsely patch'd
With diff'rent colour'd Rags, black, red, white,
   yellow,
And seem'd to speak Variety of Wretchedness.

As I was musing on this Description, and comparing it with the Object before me, the Knight told me, that this very old Woman had the Reputation of a Witch all over the Country, that her Lips were observed to be always in Motion, and that there was not a Switch about her House which her Neighbours did not believe had carried her several hundreds of Miles. If she chanced to stumble, they always found Sticks or Straws that lay in the Figure of a Cross before her. If she made any Mistake at Church, and cryed *Amen* in a wrong Place, they never failed to conclude that she was saying her Prayers backwards. There was not a Maid in the Parish that would take a Pin of her, though she should offer a Bag of Money with it. She goes by the name of *Moll White*, and has made the Country ring with several imaginary Exploits which are palmed upon her. If the Dairy-maid does not make her Butter come so soon as she should have it, *Moll White* is at the Bottom of the Churn. If a Horse sweats in the Stable, *Moll White* has been upon his Back. If a Hare makes an unexpected Escape from the Hounds, the Huntsman curses *Moll White*. Nay, (says Sir ROGER) I have known the Master of the

The Coverley Witch

Pack upon such an Occasion, send one of his Servants to see if *Moll White* has been out that Morning.

This Account raised my Curiosity so far, that I begged my Friend Sir ROGER to go with me into her hovel, which stood in a solitary Corner under the side of the Wood. Upon our first entering Sir ROGER winked to me, and pointed at something that stood behind the Door, which upon looking that Way, I found to be an old Broomstaff. At the same time he whispered me in the Ear to take notice of a Tabby Cat that sat in the Chimney-Corner, which, as the old Knight told me, lay under as bad a Report as *Moll White* herself; for besides that *Moll* is said often to accompany her in the same Shape, the Cat is reported to have spoken twice or thrice in her Life, and to have played several Pranks above the Capacity of an ordinary Cat.

I was secretly concerned to see human Nature in so much Wretchedness and Disgrace, but at the same time could not forbear smiling to hear Sir ROGER, who is a little puzzled about the old Woman, advising her as a Justice of Peace to avoid all Communication with the Devil, and never to hurt any of her Neighbour's Cattle. We concluded our Visit with a Bounty, which was very acceptable.

In our Return home, Sir ROGER told me, that old *Moll* had been often brought before him for making Children spit Pins, and giving Maids the Night-Mare; and that the Country People would be tossing

The Coverley Papers

her into a Pond and trying Experiments with her every Day, if it was not for him and his Chaplain.

I have since found upon Inquiry, that Sir ROGER was several times staggered with the Reports that had been brought him concerning this old Woman, and would frequently have bound her over to the County Sessions had not his Chaplain with much ado persuaded him to the contrary.

I have been the more particular in this Account, because I hear there is scarce a Village in *England* that has not a *Moll White* in it. When an old Woman begins to dote, and grow chargeable to a Parish, she is generally turned into a Witch, and fills the whole Country with extravagant Fancies, imaginary Distempers and terrifying Dreams. In the mean time, the poor Wretch that is the innocent Occasion of so many Evils begins to be frighted at herself, and sometimes confesses secret Commerce and Familiarities that her Imagination forms in a delirious old Age. This frequently cuts off Charity from the greatest Objects of Compassion, and inspires People with a Malevolence towards those poor decrepid Parts of our Species, in whom human Nature is defaced by Infirmity and Dotage.

Chapter XII: A Coverley Love Match

Hæret lateri lethalis arundo.
VIRGIL

THIS agreeable Seat is surrounded with so many pleasing Walks which are struck out of a Wood in the midst of which the House stands, that one can hardly ever be weary of rambling from one labyrinth of Delight to another. To one used to live in a City the Charms of the Country are so exquisite, that the Mind is lost in a certain Transport which raises us above ordinary Life, and is yet not strong enough to be inconsistent with Tranquillity. This State of Mind was I in, ravished with the Murmur of Waters, the Whisper of Breezes, the Singing of Birds; and whether I looked up to the Heavens, down on the Earth, or turned on the Prospects around me, still struck with new Sense of Pleasure; when I found by the Voice of my Friend, who walked by me, that we had insensibly strolled into the Grove sacred to the Widow. This Woman, says he, is of all others the most unintelligible; she either designs to marry, or she does not. What is the most perplexing of all, is, that she doth not either say to her Lovers she has any Resolution against that Condition of Life in general, or that she banishes them; but conscious of her own Merit she permits their Addresses without fear of any ill Consequence, or want of Respect, from their Rage or Despair. She has that in her Aspect, against which it is impossible to offend. A Man whose Thoughts are constantly built upon so agreeable an Object, must be excused if the ordinary Occurrences in Conversation are below his Attention. I call her indeed perverse, but, alas! why do I call her so? Because her superior Merit is such, that I cannot approach her without Awe, that my Heart is checked by too much Esteem: I am angry that her Charms are not more accessible, that I am more inclined to worship than salute her: How often have I wished her unhappy that I might have an Opportunity of serving her? and how often troubled in that very Imagination, at giving her the Pain of being obliged? Well I have led a miserable Life in secret upon her Account; but fancy she would have condescended to have some regard for me, if it had not been for that watchful Animal her Confidant.

Of all Persons under the Sun (continued he, calling me by my Name) be sure to set a Mark upon Confidants: they are of all People the most impertinent. What is most pleasant to observe in them, is, that they assume to themselves the Merit of the Persons whom they have in their Custody. *Orestilla* is a great Fortune, and in wonderful Danger of Surprises, therefore full of Suspicions of the least indifferent

A Coverley Love Match

thing, particularly careful of new Acquaintance, and of growing too familiar with the old. *Themista*, her favourite-Woman, is every whit as careful of whom she speaks to, and what she says. Let the Ward be a Beauty, her Confidant shall treat you with an Air of Distance; let her be a Fortune, and she assumes the suspicious Behaviour of her Friend and Patroness. Thus it is that very many of our unmarried Women of Distinction are to all Intents and Purposes married, except the Consideration of different Sexes. They are directly under the Conduct of their Whisperer; and think they are in a State of Freedom, while they can prate with one of these Attendants of all Men in general, and still avoid the Man they most like. You do not see one Heiress in a hundred whose Fate does not turn upon this Circumstance of choosing a Confidant. Thus it is that the Lady is addressed to, presented and flattered, only by Proxy, in her Woman. In my case, how is it possible that ——

Sir ROGER was proceeding in his Harangue, when he heard the Voice of one speaking very importunately, and repeating these Words, ' What, not one ' Smile?' We followed the Sound till we came to a close Thicket, on the other side of which we saw a young Woman sitting as it were in a personated Sullenness just over a transparent Fountain. Opposite to her stood Mr. *William*, Sir ROGER's Master of the Game. The Knight whispered me, ' Hist, these are Lovers.' The Huntsman looking earnestly at the Shadow of

the young Maiden in the Stream, 'Oh thou dear
' Picture, if thou couldst remain there in the Absence
' of that fair Creature, whom you represent in the
' Water, how willingly could I stand here satisfied
' for ever, without troubling my dear *Betty* herself
' with any Mention of her unfortunate *William*,
' whom she is angry with: But alas! when she pleases
' to be gone, thou wilt also vanish —— Yet let me
' talk to thee while thou dost stay. Tell my dearest
' *Betty* thou dost not more depend upon her, than
' does her *William*: Her Absence will make away
' with me as well as thee. If she offers to remove thee,
' I'll jump into these Waves to lay hold on thee; her-
' self, her own dear Person, I must never embrace
' again. —— Still do you hear me without one Smile
' —— It is too much to bear ——' He had no sooner
spoke these Words but he made an Offer of throwing
himself into the Water: At which his Mistress started
up, and at the next Instant he jumped across the
Fountain and met her in an Embrace. She half recovering from her Fright, said in the most charming
Voice imaginable, and with a Tone of Complaint,
" I thought how well you would drown yourself.
" No, no, you won't drown yourself till you have
" taken your leave of *Susan Holiday*." The Huntsman, with a Tenderness that spoke the most passionate Love, and with his Cheek close to hers, whispered
the softest Vows of Fidelity in her Ear, and cryed,
' Don't, my Dear, believe a Word *Kate Willow* says;

The Perverse Widow

A Coverley Love Match

'she is spiteful and makes Stories, because she loves
'to hear me talk to herself for your sake.'

Look you there, quoth Sir ROGER, do you see there, all Mischief comes from Confidants! But let us not interrupt them; the Maid is honest, and the Man dares not be otherwise, for he knows I loved her Father: I will interpose in this Matter, and hasten the Wedding. *Kate Willow* is a witty mischievous Wench in the Neighbourhood, who was a Beauty; and makes me hope I shall see the perverse Widow in her Condition. She was so flippant with her Answers to all the honest Fellows that came near her, and so very vain of her Beauty, that she has valued herself upon her Charms till they are ceased. She therefore now makes it her Business to prevent other young Women from being more Discreet than she was herself: However, the saucy thing said the other Day well enough, 'Sir ROGER and I must make a 'Match, for we are both despised by those we loved:' The Hussy has a great deal of Power wherever she comes, and has her Share of Cunning.

However, when I reflect upon this Woman, I do not know whether in the main I am the worse for having loved her: Whenever she is recalled to my Imagination my Youth returns, and I feel a forgotten Warmth in my Veins. This Affliction in my Life has streaked all my Conduct with a Softness, of which I should otherwise have been incapable. It is, perhaps, to this dear Image in my Heart owing, that I am apt to relent, that I easily forgive, and that many desirable things are grown into my Temper, which I should not have arrived at by better Motives than the Thought of being one Day hers. I am pretty well satisfied such a Passion as I have had is never well cured; and between you and me, I am often apt to imagine it has had some whimsical Effect upon my Brain: For I frequently find, that in my most serious Discourse I let fall some comical Familiarity of Speech or odd Phrase that makes the Company laugh; However, I cannot but allow she is a most excellent Woman. When she is in the Country I warrant she does not run into Dairies, but reads upon the Nature of Plants; but has a Glass Hive, and comes into the Garden out of Books to see them work, and observe the Policies of their Commonwealth. She understands every thing. I'd give ten Pounds to hear her argue with my Friend Sir ANDREW FREEPORT about Trade. No, no, for all she looks so innocent as it were, take my Word for it she is no Fool.

Chapter XIII: The Coverley Etiquette

Urbem quam dicunt Romam, Melibæe, putavi
Stultus ego huic nostræ similem.

VIRGIL

THE first and most obvious Reflexions which arise in a Man who changes the City for the Country, are upon the different Manners of the People whom he meets with in those two different Scenes of Life. By Manners I do not mean Morals, but Behaviour and Good-breeding as they show themselves in the Town and in the Country.

And here, in the first place, I must observe a very great Revolution that has happened in this Article of Good-breeding. Several obliging Deferences, Condescensions and Submissions, with many outward Forms and Ceremonies that accompany them, were first of all brought up among the politer Part of Mankind, who lived in Courts and Cities, and distinguished themselves from the Rustick part of the Species (who on all Occasions acted bluntly and naturally) by such a mutual Complaisance and Intercourse of Civilities. These Forms of Conversation by degrees multiplied and grew troublesome; the modish World found too great a Constraint in them, and have therefore thrown most of them aside. Conversation, like the

Romish Religion, was so encumbered with Show and Ceremony, that it stood in need of a Reformation to retrench its Superfluities, and restore it to its natural good Sense and Beauty. At present therefore an unconstrained Carriage, and a certain Openness of Behaviour, are the height of Good-breeding. The fashionable World is grown free and easy; our Manners fit more loose upon us: Nothing is so modish as an agreeable Negligence. In a word, Good-breeding shews itself most, where to an ordinary Eye it appears the least.

If after this we look on the People of Mode in the Country, we find in them the Manners of the last Age. They have no sooner fetched themselves up to the Fashion of the polite World, but the Town has dropped them, and are nearer to the first State of Nature than to those Refinements which formerly reigned in the Court, and still prevail in the Country. One may now know a Man that never conversed in the World, by his Excess of Good-breeding. A polite Country 'Squire shall make you as many Bows in half an hour, as would serve a Courtier for a Week. There is infinitely more to do about Place and Precedency in a Meeting of Justices Wives, than in an Assembly of Dutchesses.

This Rural Politeness is very troublesome to a Man of my Temper, who generally take the Chair that is next me, and walk first or last, in the Front or in the Rear, as Chance directs. I have known my Friend Sir Roger's Dinner almost cold before the

The Coverley Etiquette

Company could adjust the Ceremonial, and be prevailed upon to sit down; and have heartily pitied my old Friend, when I have seen him forced to pick and cull his Guests, as they sat at the several Parts of his Table, that he might drink their Healths according to their respective Ranks and Qualities. Honest *Will Wimble*, who I should have thought had been altogether uninfected with Ceremony, gives me abundance of Trouble in this Particular. Though he has been fishing all the Morning, he will not help himself at Dinner 'till I am served. When we are going out of the Hall, he runs behind me; and last Night, as we were walking in the Fields, stopped short at a Stile 'till I came up to it, and upon my making Signs to him to get over, told me, with a serious Smile, that sure I believed they had no Manners in the Country.

There has happened another Revolution in the Point of Good-breeding, which relates to the Conversation among Men of Mode, and which I cannot but look upon as very extraordinary. It was certainly one of the first Distinctions of a well-bred Man, to express every thing that had the most remote Appearance of being obscene, in modest Terms and distant Phrases; whilst the Clown, who had no such Delicacy of Conception and Expression, clothed his *Ideas* in those plain homely Terms that are the most obvious and natural. This kind of Good-manners was perhaps carried to an Excess, so as to make Conversation too stiff, formal, and precise: for which Reason (as Hypocrisy in one Age is generally succeeded by

Atheism in another) Conversation is in a great measure relapsed into the first Extreme; so that at present several of our Men of the Town, and particularly those who have been polished in *France*, make use of the most coarse uncivilized Words in our Language, and utter themselves often in such a manner as a Clown would blush to hear.

This infamous Piece of Good-breeding, which reigns among the Coxcombs of the Town, has not yet made its way into the Country; and as it is impossible for such an irrational way of Conversation to last long among a People that make any Profession of Religion, or Show of Modesty, if the Country Gentlemen get into it they will certainly be left in the lurch. Their Good-breeding will come too late to them, and they will be thought a Parcel of lewd Clowns, while they fancy themselves talking together like Men of Wit and Pleasure.

As the two Points of Good-breeding which I have hitherto insisted upon, regard Behaviour and Conversation, there is a third which turns upon Dress. In this too the Country are very much behind-hand. The Rural Beaus are not yet got out of the Fashion that took place at the time of the Revolution, but ride about the Country in red Coats and laced Hats, while the Women in many Parts are still trying to outvie one another in the Height of their Head-dresses.

Chapter XIV: The Coverley Ducks

Equidem credo, quia sit Divinitus illis
Ingenium.
VIRGIL

MY Friend Sir ROGER is very often merry with me upon my passing so much of my time among his Poultry. He has caught me twice or thrice looking after a Bird's Nest, and several times sitting an Hour or two together near an Hen and Chickens. He tells me he believes I am personally acquainted with every Fowl about his House; calls such a particular Cock my Favourite, and frequently complains that his Ducks and Geese have more of my Company than himself.

I must confess I am infinitely delighted with those Speculations of Nature which are to be made in a Country-Life; and as my Reading has very much lain among Books of Natural History, I cannot forbear recollecting upon this Occasion the several Remarks which I have met with in Authors, and comparing them with what falls under my own Observation: The Arguments for Providence drawn from the natural History of Animals being in my Opinion demonstrative.

It is astonishing to consider the different Degrees

83

of Care that descend from the Parent to the Young, so far as is absolutely necessary for the leaving a Posterity. Some Creatures cast their Eggs as Chance directs them, and think of them no farther, as Insects and several Kinds of Fish; others of a nicer Frame, find out proper Beds to deposit them in, and there leave them; as the Serpent, the Crocodile and the Ostrich: Others hatch their Eggs and tend the Birth, till it is able to shift for itself.

What can we call the Principle which directs every different kind of Bird to observe a particular Plan in the Structure of its Nest, and direct all the same Species to work after the same Model? It cannot be *Imitation;* for though you hatch a Crow under a Hen, and never let it see any of the Works of its own Kind, the Nest it makes shall be the same to the laying of a Stick, with all the other Nests of the same Species. It cannot be *Reason;* for were Animals indued with it to as great a Degree as Man, their Buildings would be as different as ours, according to the different Conveniences that they would propose to themselves.

Is it not remarkable, that the same Temper of Weather, which raises this genial Warmth in Animals, should cover the Trees with Leaves, and the Fields with Grass, for their Security and Concealment, and produce such infinite Swarms of Insects for the Support and Sustenance of their respective Broods?

Is it not wonderful that the Love of the Parent should be so violent while it lasts, and that it should

The Coverley Ducks

last no longer than is necessary for the Preservation of the Young?

With what Caution does the Hen provide herself a Nest in Places unfrequented, and free from Noise and Disturbance? When she has laid her Eggs in such a Manner, that she can cover them, what Care does she take in turning them frequently, that all Parts may partake of the vital Warmth? When she leaves them, to provide for her necessary Sustenance, how punctually does she return before they have time to cool, and become incapable of producing an Animal? In the Summer you see her giving herself greater Freedoms, and quitting her Care for above two Hours together; but in Winter, when the Rigour of the Season would chill the Principles of Life, and destroy the young one, she grows more assiduous in her Attendance, and stays away but half the Time. When the Birth approaches, with how much Nicety and Attention does she help the Chick to break its Prison? Not to take notice of her covering it from the Injuries of the Weather, providing it proper Nourishment, and teaching it to help itself; nor to mention her forsaking the Nest, if after the usual Time of reckoning the young one does not make its Appearance. A Chymical Operation could not be followed with greater Art or Diligence, than is seen in the hatching of a Chick; though there are many other Birds that show an infinitely greater Sagacity in all the forementioned Particulars.

But at the same time the Hen, that has all this

seeming Ingenuity, (which is indeed absolutely necessary for the Propagation of the Species,) considered in other respects, is without the least Glimmerings of Thought or common Sense. She mistakes a Piece of Chalk for an Egg, and sits upon it in the same manner: She is insensible of any Increase or Diminution in the Number of those she lays: She does not distinguish between her own and those of another Species; and when the Birth appears of never so different a Bird, will cherish it for her own. In all these Circumstances which do not carry an immediate Regard to the Subsistence of herself or her Species, she is a very Idiot.

There is not, in my Opinion, any thing more mysterious in Nature than this Instinct in Animals, which thus rises above Reason, and falls infinitely short of it. It cannot be accounted for by any Properties in Matter, and at the same time works after so odd a manner, that one cannot think it the Faculty of an intellectual Being. I look upon it as upon the Principle of Gravitation in Bodies, which is not to be explained by any known Qualities inherent in the Bodies themselves, nor from any Laws of Mechanism, but, according to the best Notions of the greatest Philosophers, is an Impression from the first Mover, and the Divine Energy acting in the Creatures.

As I was walking this Morning in the great Yard that belongs to my Friend's Country-House, I was wonderfully pleased to see the different Workings of

The Coverley Ducks

Instinct in a Hen followed by a Brood of Ducks. The Young, upon the sight of a Pond, immediately ran into it; while the Step-mother, with all imaginable Anxiety, hovered about the Borders of it, to call them out of an Element that appeared to her so dangerous and destructive. As the different Principle which acted in these different Animals cannot be termed Reason, so when we call it *Instinct*, we mean something we have no Knowledge of. To me, as I hinted in my last Paper, it seems the immediate Direction of Providence, and such an Operation of the Supreme Being, as that which determines all the Portions of Matter to their proper Centres. A modern Philosopher, quoted by Monsieur *Bayle* in his learned Dissertation on the Souls of Brutes, delivers the same Opinion, though in a bolder Form of Words, where he says, *Deus est Anima Brutorum*, God himself is the Soul of Brutes. Who can tell what to call that seeming Sagacity in Animals, which directs them to such Food as is proper for them, and makes them naturally avoid whatever is noxious or unwholsom? *Tully* has observed, that a Lamb no sooner falls from its Mother, but immediately and of his own accord applies itself to the Teat. *Dampier*, in his Travels, tells us, that when Seamen are thrown upon any of the unknown Coasts of *America*, they never venture upon the Fruit of any Tree, unless it is marked with the Pecking of Birds; but fall on without any Fear or Apprehension where the Birds have been before them.

Chapter XV: Sir Roger on the Bench

Comes jucundus in via pro vehiculo est.
PUBLIUS

A MAN'S first Care should be to avoid the Reproaches of his own Heart; his next, to escape the Censures of the World: If the last interferes with the former, it ought to be intirely neglected; but otherwise there cannot be a greater Satisfaction to an honest Mind, than to see those Approbations which it gives itself seconded by the Applauses of the Publick: A Man is more sure of his Conduct, when the Verdict which he passes upon his own Behaviour is thus warranted and confirmed by the Opinion of all that know him.

My worthy Friend Sir ROGER is one of those who is not only at Peace within himself, but beloved and esteemed by all about him. He receives a suitable Tribute for his universal Benevolence to Mankind, in the Returns of Affection and Good-will, which are paid him by every one that lives within his Neighbourhood. I lately met with two or three odd Instances of that general Respect which is shewn to the good old Knight. He would needs carry *Will Wimble* and myself with him to the County Assizes: As we were upon the Road *Will Wimble* joined a

Sir Roger on the Bench

couple of plain Men who rid before us, and conversed with them for some time; during which my Friend Sir ROGER acquainted me with their Characters.

The first of them, says he, that has a Spaniel by his Side, is a Yeoman of about an hundred Pounds a Year, an honest Man: He is just within the Game-Act, and qualified to kill an Hare or a Pheasant: He knocks down a Dinner with his Gun twice or thrice a Week; and by that means lives much cheaper than those who have not so good an Estate as himself. He would be a good Neighbour if he did not destroy so many Partridges: in short, he is a very sensible Man; shoots flying; and has been several times Foreman of the Petty Jury.

The other that rides along with him is *Tom Touchy*, a Fellow famous for *taking the Law* of every Body. There is not one in the Town where he lives that he has not sued at a Quarter-Sessions. The Rogue had once the Impudence to go to Law with the *Widow*. His Head is full of Costs, Damages, and Ejectments: He plagued a couple of honest Gentlemen so long for a Trespass in breaking one of his Hedges, till he was forced to sell the Ground it enclosed to defray the Charges of the Prosecution: His Father left him fourscore Pounds a Year; but he has *cast* and been cast so often, that he is not now worth thirty. I suppose he is going upon the old Business of the Willow-Tree.

As Sir ROGER was giving me this Account of *Tom*

The Coverley Papers

Touchy, *Will Wimble* and his two Companions stopped short till we came up to them. After having paid their Respects to Sir Roger, *Will* told him that Mr. *Touchy* and he must appeal to him upon a Dispute that arose between them. *Will* it seems had been giving his Fellow-Travellers an Account of his Angling one Day in such a Hole; when *Tom Touchy*, instead of hearing out his Story, told him that Mr. such an One, if he pleased, might *take the Law of him* for fishing in that Part of the River. My Friend Sir Roger heard them both, upon a round Trot; and after having paused some time told them, with the Air of a Man who would not give his Judgment rashly, that *much might be said on both Sides*. They were neither of them dissatisfied with the Knight's Determination, because neither of them found himself in the Wrong by it: Upon which we made the best of our Way to the Assizes.

The Court was sat before Sir Roger came; but notwithstanding all the Justices had taken their Places upon the Bench, they made room for the old Knight at the Head of them; who for his Reputation in the Country took occasion to whisper in the Judge's Ear, *That he was glad his Lordship had met with so much good Weather in his Circuit.* I was listening to the Proceeding of the Court with much Attention, and infinitely pleased with that great Appearance and Solemnity which so properly accompanies such a publick Administration of our Laws; when, after

Sir Roger on the Bench

about an Hour's Sitting, I observed to my great Surprise, in the midst of a Trial, that my Friend Sir ROGER was getting up to speak. I was in some Pain for him, till I found he had acquitted himself of two or three Sentences, with a Look of much Business and great Intrepidity.

Upon his first Rising the Court was hushed, and a general Whisper ran among the Country People that Sir ROGER *was up*. The Speech he made was so little to the Purpose, that I shall not trouble my Readers with an Account of it; and I believe was not so much designed by the Knight himself to inform the Court, as to give him a Figure in my Eye, and keep up his Credit in the Country.

I was highly delighted, when the Court rose, to see the Gentlemen of the Country gathering about my old Friend, and striving who should compliment him most; at the same time that the ordinary People gazed upon him at a distance, not a little admiring his Courage, that was not afraid to speak to the Judge.

In our Return home we met with a very odd Accident; which I cannot forbear relating, because it shews how desirous all who know Sir ROGER are of giving him Marks of their Esteem. When we were arrived upon the Verge of his Estate, we stopped at a little Inn to rest ourselves and our Horses. The Man of the House had it seems been formerly a Servant in the Knight's Family; and to do Honour to his old Master, had some time since, unknown to Sir ROGER, put him up in a Sign-post before the Door; so that *the Knight's Head* had hung out upon the Road about a Week before he himself knew any thing of the matter. As soon as Sir ROGER was acquainted with it, finding that his Servant's Indiscretion proceeded wholly from Affection and Good-will, he only told him that he had made him too high a Compliment; and when the Fellow seemed to think that could hardly be, added with a more decisive Look, That it was too great an Honour for any man under a Duke; but told him at the same time, that it might be altered with a very few Touches, and that he himself would be at the Charge of it. Accordingly they got a Painter by the Knight's Directions to add a pair of Whiskers to the Face, and by a little Aggravation of the Features to change it into the *Saracen's-Head*. I should not have known this Story had not the Innkeeper, upon Sir ROGER's alighting, told him in my Hearing, That his Honour's Head was brought back last Night with the Alterations that he had ordered to be made in it. Upon this my Friend with his usual Chearfulness related the Particulars above-mentioned, and ordered the Head to be brought into the Room. I could not forbear discovering greater Expressions of Mirth than ordinary upon the Appearance of this monstrous Face, under which, notwithstanding it was made to frown and stare in a most extraordinary manner, I could still discover a distant Resemblance of my old Friend. Sir ROGER, upon see-

Tom Touchy, a Fellow famous
for taking the Law of every Body

Sir Roger on the Bench

ing me laugh, desired me to tell him truly if I thought it possible for People to know him in that Disguise. I at first kept my usual Silence; but upon the Knight's conjuring me to tell him whether it was not still more like himself than a *Saracen*, I composed my Countenance in the best manner I could, and replied, *That much might be said on both Sides.*

These several Adventures, with the Knight's Behaviour in them, gave me as pleasant a Day as ever I met with in any of my Travels.

Chapter XVI: A Story of an Heir

Doctrina sed vim promovet insitam,
Rectique cultus pectora roborant:
Utcunque defecere mores,
Dedecorant bene nata culpe.

HORACE

AS I was Yesterday taking the Air with my Friend Sir ROGER, we were met by a fresh-coloured ruddy young Man who rid by us full Speed, with a couple of Servants behind him. Upon my Inquiry who he was, Sir ROGER told me that he was a young Gentleman of a considerable Estate, who had been educated by a tender Mother that lived not many Miles from the Place where we were. She is a very good Lady, says my Friend, but took so much care of her Son's Health that she has made him good for nothing. She quickly found that Reading was bad for his Eyes, and that Writing made his Head ake. He was let loose among the Woods as soon as he was able to ride on Horseback, or to carry a Gun upon his Shoulder. To be brief, I found, by my Friend's Account of him, that he had got a great Stock of Health, but nothing else; and that if it were a Man's Business only to live, there would not be a more accomplished young Fellow in the whole Country.

A Story of An Heir

The Truth of it is, since my residing in these Parts I have seen and heard innumerable Instances of young Heirs and elder Brothers who either from their own reflecting upon the Estates they are born to, and therefore thinking all other Accomplishments unnecessary, or from hearing these Notions frequently inculcated to them by the Flattery of their Servants and Domesticks, or from the same foolish Thought prevailing in those who have the Care of their Education, are of no manner of use but to keep up their Families, and transmit their Lands and Houses in a Line to Posterity.

This makes me often think on a Story I have heard of two Friends, which I shall give my Reader at large, under feigned Names. The Moral of it may, I hope, be useful, though there are some Circumstances which make it rather appear like a Novel, than a true Story.

Eudoxus and *Leontine* began the World with small Estates. They were both of them Men of good Sense and great Virtue. They prosecuted their Studies together in their earlier Years, and entered into such a Friendship as lasted to the end of their Lives. *Eudoxus*, at his first setting out in the World, threw himself into a Court, where by his natural Endowments and his acquired Abilities he made his way from one Post to another, till at length he had raised a very considerable Fortune. *Leontine* on the contrary sought all Opportunities of improving his Mind by Study, Conversation and Travel. He was not only acquainted with all the Sciences, but with the most eminent Professors of them throughout *Europe*. He knew perfectly well the Interests of its Princes, with the Customs and Fashions of their Courts, and could scarce meet with the Name of an extraordinary Person in the *Gazette* whom he had not either talked to or seen. In short, he had so well mixt and digested his Knowledge of Men and Books, that he made one of the most accomplished Persons of his Age. During the whole Course of his Studies and Travels he kept up a punctual Correspondence with *Eudoxus*, who often made himself acceptable to the principal Men about Court by the Intelligence which he received from *Leontine*. When they were both turned of Forty (an Age in which, according to Mr. *Cowley*, *there is no dallying with Life*) they determined, pursuant to the Resolution they had taken in the beginning of their Lives, to retire, and pass the Remainder of their Days in the Country. In order to this, they both of them married much about the same time. *Leontine*, with his own and his Wife's Fortune, bought a Farm of three hundred a Year, which lay within the Neighbourhood of his Friend *Eudoxus*, who had purchased an Estate of as many thousands. They were both of them *Fathers* about the same time, *Eudoxus* having a Son born to him, and *Leontine* a Daughter; but to the unspeakable Grief of the latter, his young Wife (in whom all his Happiness was wrapt up) died in a

A Story of An Heir

few Days after the Birth of her Daughter. His Affliction would have been insupportable, had not he been comforted by the daily Visits and Conversations of his Friend. As they were one Day talking together with their usual Intimacy, *Leontine*, considering how incapable he was of giving his Daughter a proper Education in his own House, and *Eudoxus*, reflecting on the ordinary Behaviour of a Son who knows himself to be the Heir of a great Estate, they both agreed upon an Exchange of Children, namely that the Boy should be bred up with *Leontine* as his Son, and that the Girl should live with *Eudoxus* as his Daughter, till they were each of them arrived at Years of Discretion. The Wife of *Eudoxus*, knowing that her Son could not be so advantageously brought up as under the Care of *Leontine*, and considering at the same time that he would be perpetually under her own Eye, was by Degrees prevailed upon to fall in with the Project. She therefore took *Leonilla*, for that was the Name of the Girl, and educated her as her own Daughter. The two Friends on each side had wrought themselves to such an habitual Tenderness for the Children who were under their Direction, that each of them had the real Passion of a Father, where the Title was but imaginary. *Florio*, the Name of the young Heir that lived with *Leontine*, though he had all the Duty and Affection imaginable for his supposed Parent, was taught to rejoice at the Sight of *Eudoxus*, who visited his Friend very frequently, and was dictated by his natural Affection, as well as by the Rules of Prudence, to make himself esteemed and beloved by *Florio*. The Boy was now old enough to know his supposed Father's Circumstances, and that therefore he was to make his way in the World by his own Industry. This Consideration grew stronger in him every Day, and produced so good an Effect, that he applied himself with more than ordinary Attention to the Pursuit of every thing which *Leontine* recommended to him. His natural Abilities, which were very good, assisted by the Directions of so excellent a Counsellor, enabled him to make a quicker Progress than ordinary through all the Parts of his Education. Before he was twenty Years of Age, having finished his Studies and Exercises with great Applause, he was removed from the University to the Inns of Court, where there are very few that make themselves considerable Proficients in the Studies of the Place, who know they shall arrive at great Estates without them. This was not *Florio's* Case; he found that three hundred a Year was but a poor Estate for *Leontine* and himself to live upon, so that he studied without Intermission till he gained a very good Insight into the Constitution and Laws of his Country.

I should have told my Reader, that whilst *Florio* lived at the House of his Foster-father he was always an acceptable Guest in the Family of *Eudoxus*, where he became acquainted with *Leonilla* from her Infancy. His Acquaintance with her by degrees grew

A Story of An Heir

into Love, which in a Mind trained up in all the Sentiments of Honour and Virtue became a very uneasy Passion. He despaired of gaining an Heiress of so great a Fortune, and would rather have died than attempted it by any indirect Methods. *Leonilla*, who was a Woman of the greatest Beauty joined with the greatest Modesty, entertained at the same time a secret Passion for *Florio*, but conducted herself with so much Prudence that she never gave him the least Intimation of it. *Florio* was now engaged in all those Arts and Improvements that are proper to raise a Man's private Fortune, and give him a Figure in his Country, but secretly tormented with that Passion which burns with the greatest Fury in a virtuous and noble Heart, when he received a sudden Summons from *Leontine* to repair to him in the Country the next Day. For it seems *Eudoxus* was so filled with the Report of his Son's Reputation, that he could no longer withhold making himself known to him. The Morning after his Arrival at the House of his supposed Father, *Leontine* told him that *Eudoxus* had something of great Importance to communicate to him; upon which the good Man embraced him and wept. *Florio* was no sooner arrived at the great House that stood in his Neighbourhood, but *Eudoxus* took him by the Hand, after the first Salutes were over, and conducted him into his Closet. He there opened to him the whole Secret of his Parentage and Education, concluding after this manner: *I have no other way left of acknowledging my Gratitude to* Leontine, *than by marrying you to his Daughter. He shall not lose the Pleasure of being your Father by the Discovery I have made to you.* Leonilla *too shall be still my Daughter; her filial Piety, though misplaced, has been so exemplary that it deserves the greatest Reward I can confer upon it. You shall have the Pleasure of seeing a great Estate fall to you, which you would have lost the Relish of had you known yourself born to it. Continue only to deserve it in the same manner you did before you were possessed of it. I have left your Mother in the next Room. Her Heart yearns towards you. She is making the same Discoveries to* Leonilla *which I have made to yourself. Florio was so overwhelmed with this Profusion of Happiness, that he was not able to make a Reply, but threw himself down at his Father's Feet, and amidst a Flood of Tears, kissed and embraced his Knees, asking his Blessing, and expressing in dumb Show those Sentiments of Love, Duty, and Gratitude that were too big for Utterance. To conclude, the happy Pair were married, and half* Eudoxus's *Estate settled upon them.* Leontine *and* Eudoxus *passed the Remainder of their Lives together; and received in the dutiful and affectionate Behaviour of* Florio *and* Leonilla *the just Recompence, as well as the natural Effects, of that Care which they had bestowed upon them in their Education.*

Chapter XVII: Sir Roger and Party Spirit

Ne, pueri, ne tanta animis assuescite bella:
Neu patriæ validas in viscera vertite vires.
VIRGIL

MY worthy Friend Sir ROGER, when we are talking of the Malice of Parties, very frequently tells us an Accident that happened to him when he was a School-boy, which was at a time when the Feuds ran high between the Round-heads and Cavaliers. This worthy Knight, being then but a Stripling, had occasion to inquire which was the Way to St. *Anne's* Lane, upon which the Person whom he spoke to, instead of answering his Question, called him a young Popish Cur, and asked him who had made *Anne* a Saint! The Boy, being in some Confusion, inquired of the next he met, which was the Way to *Anne's* Lane; but was called a prick-eared Cur for his Pains, and instead of being shewn the Way, was told that she had been a Saint before he was born, and would be one after he was hanged. Upon this, says Sir ROGER, I did not think fit to repeat the former Question, but going into every Lane of the Neighbourhood, asked what they called the Name of that Lane. By which ingenious Artifice he found out the Place he inquired after, without giving Offence to any Party. Sir ROGER generally closes this Narrative with Reflexions on the Mischief that Parties do in the Country; how they spoil good Neighbourhood, and make honest Gentlemen hate one another; besides that they manifestly tend to the prejudice of the Land-Tax, and the Destruction of the Game.

There cannot a greater Judgment befal a Country than such a dreadful Spirit of Division as rends a Government into two distinct People, and makes them greater Strangers and more averse to one another, than if they were actually two different Nations. The Effects of such a Division are pernicious to the last degree, not only with regard to those Advantages which they give the Common Enemy, but to those private Evils which they produce in the Heart of almost every particular Person. This Influence is very fatal both to Mens Morals and their Understandings; it sinks the Virtue of a Nation, and not only so, but destroys even Common Sense.

A furious Party Spirit, when it rages in its full Violence, exerts itself in Civil War and Bloodshed; and when it is under its greatest Restraints naturally breaks out in Falshood, Detraction, Calumny, and a partial Administration of Justice. In a word, it fills a Nation with Spleen and Rancour, and extinguishes all the Seeds of Good-nature, Compassion, and Humanity.

I remember to have read in *Diodorus Siculus* an Account of a very active little Animal, which I think he calls the *Ichneumon*, that makes it the whole Business of his Life to break the Eggs of the Crocodile, which he is always in search after. This Instinct is the more remarkable, because the *Ichneumon* never feeds upon the Eggs he has broken, nor any other Way finds his Account in them. Were it not for the Incessant Labours of this industrious Animal, *Ægypt*, says the Historian, would be over-run with Crocodiles; for the *Ægyptians* are so far from destroying those pernicious Creatures, that they worship them as Gods.

If we look into the Behaviour of ordinary Partizans, we shall find them far from resembling this disinterested Animal; and rather acting after the Example of the wild *Tartars*, who are ambitious of destroying a Man of the most extraordinary Parts and Accomplishments, as thinking that upon his Decease the same Talents, whatever Post they qualified him for, enter of Course into his Destroyer.

As in the whole Train of my Speculations, I have endeavoured as much as I am able to extinguish that pernicious Spirit of Passion and Prejudice, which rages with the same Violence in all Parties, I am still the more desirous of doing some Good in this Particular, because I observe that the Spirit of Party reigns more in the Country than in the Town. It here contracts a kind of Brutality and rustic Fierceness, to which Men of a politer Conversation are wholly Strangers. It extends itself even to the Return of the

Bow and the Hat; and at the same time that the Heads of Parties preserve towards one another an outward Show of Good-breeding, and keep up a perpetual Intercourse of Civilities, their Tools that are dispersed in these outlying Parts will not so much as mingle together at a Cock-match. This Humour fills the Country with several periodical Meetings of Whig Jockies and Tory Fox-hunters; not to mention the innumerable Curses, Frowns, and Whispers it produces at a Quarter-Sessions.

 I do not know whether I have observed in any of my former Papers, that my Friends Sir ROGER DE COVERLEY and Sir ANDREW FREEPORT are of different Principles, the first of them inclined to the *landed* and the other to the *monied* Interest. This Humour is so moderate in each of them, that it proceeds no farther than to an agreeable Rallery, which very often diverts the rest of the Club. I find however that the Knight is a much stronger Tory in the Country than in Town, which, as he has told me in my Ear, is absolutely necessary for the keeping up his Interest. In all our Journey from *London* to his House we did not so much as bait at a Whig-Inn; or if by chance the Coachman stopped at a wrong Place, one of Sir ROGER's Servants would ride up to his Master full Speed, and whisper to him that the Master of the House was against such an one in the last Election. This often betrayed us into hard Beds and bad Cheer; for we were not so inquisitive about the Inn as the

Sir Roger and Party Spirit

Inn-keeper; and, provided our Landlord's Principles were sound, did not take any Notice of the Staleness of his Provisions. This I found still the more inconvenient, because the better the Host was, the worse generally were his Accommodations; the Fellow knowing very well that those who were his Friends would take up with coarse Diet and an hard Lodging. For these Reasons, all the while I was upon the Road I dreaded entering into an House of any one that Sir ROGER had applauded for an honest Man.

Since my Stay at Sir ROGER's in the Country, I daily find more Instances of this narrow Party-Humour. Being upon a Bowling-green at a Neighbouring Market-Town the other Day, (for that is the Place where the Gentlemen of one Side meet once a Week) I observed a Stranger among them of a better Presence and genteeler Behaviour than ordinary; but was much surprised, that notwithstanding he was a very fair *Better*, no Body would take him up. But upon Inquiry I found, that he was one who had given a disagreeable Vote in a former Parliament, for which Reason there was not a Man upon that Bowling-green who would have so much Correspondence with him as to win his Money of him.

Among other instances of this Nature, I must not omit one which concerns myself. *Will Wimble* was the other Day relating several strange Stories that he had picked up no Body knows where of a certain great Man; and upon my staring at him, as one that was surprised to hear such Things in the Country, which had never been so much as whispered in the Town, *Will* stopped short in the Thread of his Discourse, and after Dinner asked my Friend Sir ROGER in his Ear if he was sure that I was not a Fanatick.

It gives me a serious Concern to see such a Spirit of Dissension in the Country; not only as it destroys Virtue and common Sense, and renders us in a manner Barbarians towards one another, but as it perpetuates our Animosities, widens our Breaches, and transmits our present Passions and Prejudices to our Posterity. For my own part, I am sometimes afraid that I discover the Seeds of a Civil War in these our Divisions; and therefore cannot but bewail, as in their first Principles, the Miseries and Calamities of our Children.

Chapter XVIII: On Gipseys in General

*Semperque recentes
Convectare juvat prædas, & vivere rapto.*
VIRGIL

As I was Yesterday riding out in the Fields with my Friend Sir ROGER, we saw there at a little Distance from us a Troop of Gipsies. Upon the first Discovery of them, my Friend was in some doubt whether we should not exert the *Justice of the Peace* upon such a Band of Lawless Vagrants; but not having his Clerk with him, who is a necessary Counsellor on these Occasions, and fearing that his Poultry might fare the worse for it, he let the Thought drop: But at the same time gave me a particular Account of the Mischiefs they do in the Country, in stealing People's Goods and spoiling their Servants. If a stray Piece of Linen hangs upon an Hedge, says Sir ROGER, they are sure to have it; if the Hog loses his Way in the Fields, it is ten to one but he becomes their Prey; our Geese cannot live in Peace for them; if a Man prosecutes them with Severity, his Hen-roost is sure to pay for it: They generally straggle into these Parts about this Time of the Year; and set the Heads of our Servant-Maids so agog for Husbands, that we do not expect to have any Business done as it should be whilst they are in the Country. I have an honest Dairymaid who crosses their Hands with a Piece of Silver every Summer, and never fails being promised the handsomest young Fellow in the Parish for her pains. Your Friend the Butler has been Fool enough to be seduced by them; and, though he is sure to lose a Knife, a Fork, or a Spoon every time his Fortune is told him, generally shuts himself up in the Pantry with an old Gipsy for above half an Hour once in a Twelvemonth. Sweet-hearts are the things they live upon, which they bestow very plentifully upon all those that apply themselves to them. You see now and then some handsom young Jades among them: The Sluts have very often white Teeth and black Eyes.

Sir ROGER observing that I listened with great Attention to his Account of a People who were so intirely new to me, told me, That if I would they should tell us our Fortunes. As I was very well pleased with the Knight's Proposal, we rid up and communicated our Hands to them. A *Cassandra* of the Crew, after having examined my Lines very diligently, told me, That I loved a pretty Maid in a Corner, that I was a good Woman's Man, with some other Particulars which I do not think proper to relate. My Friend Sir ROGER alighted from his Horse, and exposing his Palm to two or three that stood by him, they crumpled it into all Shapes, and diligently scanned every Wrinkle that could be made in it; when one of them, who was older and more Sun-burnt than the rest,

On Gypseys in General

told him, that he had a Widow in his Line of Life: Upon which the Knight cried, Go, go, you are an idle Baggage; and at the same time smiled upon me. The Gipsey finding he was not displeased in his Heart, told him, after a farther Inquiry into his Hand, that his True-love was constant, and that she should dream of him to-night: My old Friend cried Pish, and bid her go on. The Gipsey told him that he was a Bachelor, but would not be so long; and that he was dearer to somebody than he thought: The Knight still repeated She was an idle Baggage, and bid her go on. Ah Master, says the Gipsey, that roguish Leer of yours makes a pretty Woman's Heart ake; you han't that Simper about the Mouth for nothing—— The uncouth Gibberish with which all this was uttered like the Darkness of an Oracle, made us the more attentive to it. To be short, the Knight left the Money with her that he had crossed her Hand with, and got up again on his Horse.

As we were riding away, Sir ROGER told me, that he knew several sensible People who believed these Gipseys now and then foretold very strange things; and for half an Hour together appeared more jocund than ordinary. In the Height of his Good-humour, meeting a common Beggar upon the Road who was no Conjurer, as he went to relieve him he found his Pocket was picked: That being a Kind of Palmistry at which this Race of Vermin are very dexterous.

Chapter XIX: *A Summons to London*

Ipsæ rursum concedite Sylvæ.
VIRGIL

IT is usual for a Man who loves Country Sports to preserve the Game in his own Grounds, and divert himself upon those that belong to his Neighbour. My Friend Sir ROGER generally goes two or three Miles from his House, and gets into the Frontiers of his Estate, before he beats about in search of a Hare or Partridge, on purpose to spare his own Fields, where he is always sure of finding Diversion when the worst comes to the worst. By this Means the Breed about his House has time to increase and multiply, besides that the Sport is the more agreeable where the Game is the harder to come at, and where it does not lie so thick as to produce any Perplexity or Confusion in the Pursuit. For these Reasons the Country Gentleman like the Fox, seldom preys near his own Home.

In the same manner I have made a Month's Excursion out of the Town, which is the great Field of Game for Sportsmen of my Species, to try my Fortune in the Country, where I have started several Subjects, and hunted them down, with some Pleasure to myself, and I hope to others. I am here forced to

A Summons to London

use a great deal of Diligence before I can spring anything to my Mind, whereas in Town, whilst I am following one Character, it is ten to one but I am crossed in my Way by another, and put up such a Variety of odd Creatures in both Sexes, that they foil the Scent of one another, and puzzle the Chace. My greatest Difficulty in the Country is to find Sport, and in Town to choose it. In the mean time, as I have given a whole Month's Rest to the Cities of *London* and *Westminster*, I promise myself abundance of new Game upon my return thither.

It is indeed high time for me to leave the Country, since I find the whole Neighbourhood begin to grow very inquisitive after my Name and Character: My Love of Solitude, Taciturnity, and particular way of Life, having raised a great Curiosity in all these Parts.

The Notions which have been framed of me are various; some look upon me as very proud, some as very modest, and some as very melancholy. *Will Wimble*, as my Friend the Butler tells me, observing me very much alone, and extremely silent when I am in Company, is afraid I have killed a Man. The Country People seem to suspect me for a Conjurer; and some of them hearing of the Visit which I made to *Moll White*, will needs have it that Sir ROGER has brought down a Cunning Man with him, to cure the old Woman, and free the Country from her Charms. So that the Character which I go under in part of the Neighbourhood, is what they here call a *White Witch.*

A Justice of Peace, who lives about five Miles off, and is not of Sir ROGER's Party, has it seems said twice or thrice at his Table, that he wishes Sir ROGER does not harbour a Jesuit in his House, and that he thinks the Gentlemen of the Country would do very well to make me give some Account of myself.

On the other side, some of Sir ROGER's Friends are afraid the old Knight is imposed upon by a designing Fellow, and as they have heard that he converses very promiscuously, when he is in Town, do not know but he has brought down with him some discarded Whig, that is sullen and says nothing because he is out of Place.

Such is the Variety of Opinions which are here entertained of me, so that I pass among some for a disaffected Person, and among others for a Popish Priest, among some for a Wizard, and among others for a Murderer; and all this for no other Reason, that I can imagine, but because I do not hoot and hollow and make a Noise. It is true my Friend Sir ROGER tells them, *That it is my way*, and that I am only a Philosopher; but this will not satisfy them. They think there is more in me than he discovers, and that I do not hold my Tongue for nothing.

For these and other Reasons I shall set out for *London* to-morrow, having found by Experience that the Country is not a Place for a Person of my Tem-

A Summons to London

per, who does not love jollity, and what they call good Neighbourhood. A Man that is out of Humour when an unexpected Guest breaks in upon him, and does not care for sacrificing an Afternoon to every Chance-comer; that will be the Master of his own Time, and the Pursuer of his own Inclinations, makes but a very unsociable Figure in this kind of Life. I shall therefore retire into the Town, if I may make use of that Phrase, and get into the Crowd again as fast as I can in order to be alone. I can there raise what Speculations I please upon others without being observed myself, and at the same time enjoy all the Advantages of Company with all the Privileges of Solitude. In the mean while, to finish the Month and conclude these my rural Speculations, I shall here insert a Letter from my Friend WILL HONEYCOMB, who has not lived a Month for these forty Years out of the Smoke of *London*, and rallies me after his way upon my Country Life.

Dear SPEC,

'I Suppose this Letter will find thee picking of
' Daisies, or smelling to a Lock of Hay, or passing
' away thy time in some innocent Country Diver-
' sion of the like Nature. I have however Orders
' from the Club to summon thee up to Town, being
' all of us cursedly afraid thou wilt not be able to
' relish our Company, after thy Conversations with
' *Moll White* and *Will Wimble*. Pr'ythee don't send

'us up any more Stories of a Cock and a Bull, nor
' frighten the Town with Spirits and Witches. Thy
' Speculations begin to smell confoundedly of Woods
' and Meadows. If thou dost not come up quickly,
' we shall conclude that thou art in Love with one of
' Sir ROGER's Dairy-Maids. Service to the Knight.
' Sir ANDREW is grown the Cock of the Club since he
' left us, and if he does not return quickly will make
' every Mother's Son of us Commonwealth's Men.

Dear SPEC, *Thine Eternally*,
WILL HONEYCOMB.

Chapter XX: Farewell to Coverley Hall

Qui, aut Tempus quid postulet non videt, aut plura loquitur, aut se ostentat, aut eorum quibuscum est rationem non habet, is ineptus esse dicitur.
TULLIUS

HAVING notified to my good Friend Sir ROGER that I should set out for *London* the next Day, his Horses were ready at the appointed Hour in the Evening; and attended by one of his Grooms, I arrived at the County-Town at Twilight, in order to be ready for the Stage-coach the Day following. As soon as we arrived at the Inn, the Servant, who waited upon me, inquired of the Chamberlain in my Hearing what Company he had for the Coach? The Fellow answered, Mrs. *Betty Arable* the great Fortune, and the Widow her Mother; a recruiting Officer (who took a Place because they were to go;) young Squire *Quickset* her Cousin (that her Mother wished her to be married to;) *Ephraim* the Quaker, her Guardian; and a Gentleman that had studied himself dumb from Sir ROGER DE COVERLEY's. I observed by what he said of myself, that according to his Office he dealt much in Intelligence; and doubted not but there was some Foundation for his Reports for the rest of the Company, as well as for the whimsical Account he gave of me.

115

The next Morning just at Day-break we were all called; and I, who know my own natural shyness, and endeavour to be as little liable to be disputed with as possible, dressed immediately, that I might make no one wait. The first Preparation for our Setting out was, that the Captain's Half-Pike was placed near the Coachman, and a Drum behind the Coach. In the mean time the Drummer, the Captain's Equipage, was very loud, that none of the Captain's Things should be placed so as to be spoiled; upon which his Cloke-bag was fixed in the Seat of the Coach: and the Captain himself, according to a frequent, though invidious Behaviour of Military Men, ordered his Men to look sharp, that none but one of the Ladies should have the Place he had taken fronting to the Coach-box.

We were in some little time fixed in our Seats, and sat with that dislike which People not too good-natured usually conceive of each other at first Sight. The Coach jumbled us insensibly into some sort of Familiarity: and we had not moved above two Miles, when the Widow asked the Captain what Success he had in his Recruiting? The Officer with a Frankness he believed very graceful, told her, ' That indeed he ' had but very little Luck, and had suffered much by ' Desertion, therefore should be glad to end his ' Warfare in the Service of her or her fair Daughter. ' In a word,' continued he, ' I am a Soldier, and to ' be plain is my Character: You see me, Madam,

The invidious
Behavior of Military Men

Farewell to Coverley Hall

' young, sound, and also impudent; take me yourself,
' Widow, or give me to her, I will be wholly at your
' Disposal. I am a Soldier of Fortune, ha!' This was
followed by a vain Laugh of his own, and a deep
Silence of all the rest of the Company. I had nothing
left for it but to fall fast asleep, which I did with all
Speed. 'Come,' said he, 'resolve upon it, we will
' make a Wedding at the next Town: We will wake
' this pleasant Companion who is fallen asleep, to be
' the Brideman, and' (giving the Quaker a Clap on
the Knee) he concluded, ' This sly Saint, who, I'll
' warrant, understands what's what as well as you or
' I, Widow, shall give the Bride as Father.'

The Quaker, who happened to be a Man of Smartness, answered, ' Friend, I take it in good part, that
' thou hast given me the Authority of a Father over
' this comely and virtuous Child; and I must assure
' thee, that if I have the giving her, I shall not bestow
' her on thee. Thy Mirth, Friend, savoureth of
' Folly: Thou art a Person of a light Mind; thy
' Drum is a Type of thee, it soundeth because it is
' empty. Verily it is not from thy Fulness, but thy
' Emptiness that thou hast spoken this Day. Friend,
' Friend, we have hired this Coach in Partnership
' with thee, to carry us to the great City; we cannot
' go any other Way. This worthy Mother must hear
' thee if thou wilt needs utter thy Follies; we cannot
' help it, Friend, I say: if thou wilt, we must hear
' thee: But if thou wert a Man of Understanding,

'thou wouldst not take Advantage of thy courageous
'Countenance to abash us Children of Peace. Thou
'art, thou sayest, a Soldier; give Quarter to us, who
'cannot resist thee. Why didst thou fleer at our
'Friend, who feigned himself asleep? he said noth-
'ing; but how dost thou know what he containeth?
'If thou speakest improper things in the Hearing of
'this virtuous young Virgin, consider it as an Out-
'rage against a distressed Person that cannot get from
'thee: To speak indiscreetly what we are obliged to
'hear, by being hasped up with thee in this publick
'Vehicle, is in some degree assaulting on the high
'Road.'

Here *Ephraim* paused, and the Captain with an happy and uncommon Impudence (which can be convicted and support itself at the same time) cries, 'Faith, Friend, I thank thee; I should have been a 'little impertinent if thou hadst not reprimanded me. 'Come, thou art, I see, a smoky old Fellow, and I'll 'be very orderly the ensuing Part of my Journey. I 'was going to give myself Airs, but, Ladies, I beg 'Pardon.'

The Captain was so little out of Humour, and our Company was so far from being soured by this little Ruffle, that *Ephraim* and he took a particular Delight in being agreeable to each other for the future; and assumed their different Provinces in the Conduct of the Company. Our Reckonings, Apartments, and Accommodation, fell under *Ephraim:* and the Cap-

Farewell to Coverley Hall

tain looked to all Disputes on the Road, as the good Behaviour of our Coachman, and the right we had of taking Place as going to *London* of all Vehicles coming from thence.

The Occurrences we met with were ordinary, and very little happened which could entertain by the Relation of them: But when I considered the Company we were in, I took it for no small Good-fortune that the whole Journey was not spent in Impertinences, which to the one Part of us might be an Entertainment, to the other a Suffering.

What therefore *Ephraim* said when we were almost arrived at *London*, had to me an Air not only of good Understanding but good Breeding. Upon the young Lady's expressing her Satisfaction in the Journey, and declaring how delightful it had been to her, *Ephraim* delivered himself as follows: ' There is no
' ordinary Part of human Life which expresseth so
' much a good Mind, and a right inward Man, as his
' Behaviour upon meeting with Strangers, especially
' such as may seem the most unsuitable Companions
' to him: Such a Man, when he falleth in the way
' with Persons of Simplicity and Innocence, however
' knowing he may be in the Ways of Men, will not
' vaunt himself thereof; but will the rather hide his
' Superiority to them, that he may not be painful unto
' them. My good Friend, (continued he, turning to
' the Officer) thee and I are to part by and by, and
' peradventure we may never meet again: But be ad-

The Coverley Papers

'vised by a plain Man; Modes and Apparel are but
'Trifles to the real Man, therefore do not think such
'a Man as thyself terrible for thy Garb, nor such a
'one as me contemptible for mine. When two such
'as thee and I meet, with Affections as we ought to
'have towards each other, thou shouldst rejoice to
'see my peaceable Demeanour, and I should be glad
'to see thy Strength and Ability to protect me in it.'

Chapter XXI: Sir Roger in London

Aevo rarissima nostro
Simplicitas.
                    OVID

I WAS this Morning surprised with a great knocking at the Door, when my Landlady's Daughter came up to me, and told me, that there was a Man below desired to speak with me. Upon my asking her who it was, she told me it was a very grave elderly Person, but that she did not know his Name. I immediately went down to him, and found him to be the Coachman of my worthy Friend Sir ROGER DE COVERLEY. He told me that his Master came to Town last Night, and would be glad to take a Turn with me in *Gray's-Inn* Walks. As I was wondering in myself what had brought Sir ROGER to Town, not having lately received any Letter from him, he told me that his Master was come up to get a Sight of Prince *Eugene*, and that he desired I would meet him.

I was not a little pleased with the Curiosity of the old Knight, though I did not much wonder at it, having heard him say more than once in private Discourse, that he looked upon Prince *Eugenio* (for so the Knight always calls him) to be a greater Man than *Scanderbeg*.

The Coverley Papers

I was no sooner come into *Gray's-Inn* Walks, but I heard my Friend upon the Terrace hemming twice or thrice to himself with great Vigour, for he loves to clear his Pipes in good Air (to make use of his own Phrase), and is not a little pleased with any one who takes notice of the Strength which he still exerts in his Morning Hemms.

I was touched with a secret Joy at the Sight of the good old Man, who before he saw me was engaged in Conversation with a Beggar-Man that had asked an Alms of him. I could hear my Friend chide him for not finding out some Work; but at the same time saw him put his Hand in his Pocket and give him Six-pence.

Our Salutations were very hearty on both Sides, consisting of many kind Shakes of the Hand, and several affectionate Looks which we cast upon one another. After which the Knight told me my good Friend his Chaplain was very well, and much at my Service, and that the *Sunday* before he had made a most incomparable Sermon out of Doctor *Barrow*. I have left, says he, all my Affairs in his Hands, and being willing to lay an Obligation upon him, have deposited with him thirty Marks, to be distributed among his poor Parishioners.

He then proceeded to acquaint me with the Welfare of *Will Wimble*. Upon which he put his Hand into his Fob and presented me in his Name with a Tobacco-Stopper, telling me that *Will* had been busy all the Beginning of the Winter, in turning great Quantities of them; and that he made a Present of one to every Gentleman in the Country who has good Principles, and smokes. He added, that poor *Will* was at present under great Tribulation, for that *Tom Touchy* had taken the Law of him for cutting some Hazel Sticks out of one of his Hedges.

Among other Pieces of News which the Knight brought from his Country Seat, he informed me that *Moll White* was dead; and that about a Month after her Death the Wind was so very high, that it blew down the End of one of his Barns. But for my own Part, says Sir Roger, I do not think that the old Woman had any Hand in it.

He afterwards fell into an Account of the Diversions which had passed in his House during the Holidays; for Sir Roger, after the laudable Custom of his Ancestors, always keeps open House at *Christmas*. I learned from him, that he had killed eight fat Hogs for this Season, that he had dealt about his Chines very liberally amongst his Neighbours, and that in particular he had sent a string of Hogs-puddings with a pack of Cards to every poor Family in the Parish. I have often thought, says Sir Roger, it happens very well that *Christmas* should fall out in the middle of Winter. It is the most dead uncomfortable Time of the Year, when the poor People would suffer very much from their Poverty and Cold, if they had not good Cheer, warm Fires, and *Christmas* Gambols to support them. I love to rejoice their poor Hearts at this season, and to see the whole Village merry in my great Hall. I allow a double Quantity of Malt to my small Beer, and set it a running for twelve Days to every one that calls for it. I have always a Piece of cold Beef and a Mince-Pye upon the Table, and am wonderfully pleased to see my Tenants pass away a whole Evening in playing their innocent Tricks, and smutting one another. Our Friend *Will Wimble* is as merry as any of them, and shows a thousand roguish Tricks upon these Occasions.

I was very much delighted with the Reflexion of my old Friend, which carried so much Goodness in it. He then lanched out into the Praise of the late Act of Parliament for securing the Church of *England*, and told me, with great Satisfaction, that he believed it already began to take Effect, for that a rigid Dissenter, who chanced to dine at his House on *Christmas* Day, had been observed to eat very plentifully of his Plum-porridge.

After having dispatched all our Country Matters, Sir ROGER made several Inquiries concerning the Club, and particularly of his old Antagonist Sir ANDREW FREEPORT. He asked me with a kind of a Smile, whether Sir ANDREW had not taken the Advantage of his Absence, to vent among them some of his Republican Doctrines; but soon after gathering up his Countenance into a more than ordinary Seriousness, Tell me truly, says he, don't you think Sir

Sir Roger in London

ANDREW had a Hand in the Pope's Procession——but without giving me time to answer him, Well, well, says he, I know you are a wary Man, and do not care to talk of publick Matters.

The Knight then asked me, if I had seen Prince *Eugenio*, and made me promise to get him a Stand in some convenient Place where he might have a full Sight of that extraordinary Man, whose Presence does so much Honour to the *British* Nation. He dwelt very long on the Praises of this Great General, and I found that, since I was with him in the Country, he had drawn many Observations together out of his reading in *Baker's* Chronicle, and other Authors, who always lie in his Hall Window, which very much redound to the Honour of this Prince.

Having passed away the greatest Part of the Morning in hearing the Knight's Reflexions, which were partly private, and partly political, he asked me if I would smoke a Pipe with him over a Dish of Coffee at *Squire's*. As I love the old Man, I take Delight in complying with every thing that is agreeable to him, and accordingly waited on him to the Coffee-house, where his venerable Figure drew upon us the Eyes of the whole Room. He had no sooner seated himself at the upper End of the high Table, but he called for a clean Pipe, a Paper of Tobacco, a Dish of Coffee, a Wax-Candle, and the *Supplement*, with such an Air of Chearfulness and Good-humour, that all the Boys in the Coffee-room (who seemed to take pleasure in serving him) were at once employed on his several Errands, insomuch that no Body else could come at a Dish of Tea, till the Knight had got all his Conveniences about him.

Chapter XXII: Sir Roger in Westminster Abbey

Ire tamen restat, Numa quò devenit, et Ancus.
HORACE

MY Friend Sir ROGER DE COVERLEY told me t'other Night, that he had been reading my Paper upon *Westminster Abbey*, in which, says he, there are a great many ingenious Fancies. He told me at the same time, that he observed I had promised another Paper upon *the Tombs*, and that he should be glad to go and see them with me, not having visited them since he had read History. I could not at first imagine how this came into the Knight's Head, till I recollected that he had been very busy all last Summer upon *Baker's* Chronicle, which he has quoted several times in his Disputes with Sir ANDREW FREEPORT since his last coming to Town. Accordingly I promised to call upon him the next Morning, that we might go together to the *Abbey*.

I found the Knight under his Butler's Hands, who always shaves him. He was no sooner Dressed, than he called for a Glass of the Widow *Trueby's* Water, which he told me he always drank before he went abroad. He recommended to me a Dram of it at the same time, with so much Heartiness, that I could not forbear drinking it. As soon as I had got it down, I found it very unpalatable; upon which the Knight observing that I had made several wry Faces, told me that he knew I should not like it at first, but that it was the best thing in the World against the Stone or Gravel.

I could have wished indeed that he had acquainted me with the Virtues of it sooner; but it was too late to complain, and I knew what he had done was out of Good-will. Sir ROGER told me further, that he looked upon it to be very good for a Man whilst he staid in Town, to keep off Infection, and that he got together a Quantity of it upon the first News of the Sickness being at *Dantzick:* When of a sudden turning short to one of his Servants, who stood behind him, he bid him call a Hackney-Coach, and take care it was an elderly Man that drove it.

He then resumed his Discourse upon Mrs. *Trueby's* Water, telling me that the Widow *Trueby* was one who did more good than all the Doctors and Apothecaries in the Country: That she distilled every Poppy that grew within five Miles of her; that she distributed her Water *gratis* among all sorts of People; to which the Knight added, that she had a very great Jointure, and that the whole Country would fain have it a Match between him and her; and truly, says Sir ROGER, if I had not been engaged, perhaps I could not have done better.

His Discourse was broken off by his Man's telling him he had called a Coach. Upon our going to it, after having cast his Eye upon the Wheels, he asked the Coachman if his Axletree was good; upon the Fellow's telling him he would warrant it, the Knight turned to me, told me he looked like an honest Man, and went in without further Ceremony.

We had not gone far, when Sir ROGER, popping out his Head, called the Coachman down from his Box, and, upon his presenting himself at the Window, asked him if he smoked; as I was considering what this would end in, he bid him stop by the way at any good Tobacconist's, and take in a Roll of their best *Virginia*. Nothing material happened in the remaining Part of our Journey, till we were set down at the West-end of the *Abbey*.

As we went up the Body of the Church, the Knight pointed at the Trophies upon one of the new Monuments, and cryed out, A brave Man I warrant him! Passing afterwards by Sir *Cloudsly Shovel*, he flung his hand that way, and cryed, Sir *Cloudsly Shovel!* a very gallant Man! As we stood before *Busby's* Tomb, the Knight uttered himself again after the same Manner, Dr. *Busby*, a great Man! he whipped my Grandfather; a very great Man! I should have gone to him myself, if I had not been a Blockhead; a very great Man!

We were immediately conducted into the little Chapel on the right hand. Sir ROGER, planting himself at our Historian's Elbow, was very attentive to every thing he said, particularly to the Account he gave us of the Lord who had cut off the King of *Morocco's* Head. Among several other Figures, he was very well pleased to see the Statesman *Cecil* upon his Knees; and concluding them all to be great Men, was conducted to the Figure which represents that Martyr to good Housewifry, who died by the prick of a Needle. Upon our Interpreter's telling us, that she was a Maid of Honour to Queen *Elizabeth*, the Knight was very inquisitive into her Name and Family; and after having regarded her Finger for some time, I wonder, says he, that Sir *Richard Baker* has said nothing of her in his Chronicle.

We were then conveyed to the two Coronation Chairs, where my old Friend, after having heard that the Stone underneath the most ancient of them, which was brought from *Scotland*, was called *Jacob's Pillar*, sat himself down in the Chair; and looking like the Figure of an old *Gothick* King, asked our Interpreter, what Authority they had to say, that *Jacob* had ever been in *Scotland?* The Fellow, instead of returning him an Answer, told him, that he hoped his Honour would pay his Forfeit. I could observe Sir ROGER a little ruffled upon being thus trepanned; but our Guide not insisting upon his Demand, the Knight soon recovered his good-humour and whispered in my Ear, that if WILL WIMBLE were with us, and saw those two Chairs, it would go hard but he would get a Tobacco-Stopper out of one or t'other of them.

Sir Roger in Westminster Abbey

Sir ROGER, in the next Place, laid his hand upon *Edward* the Third's Sword, and leaning upon the Pommel of it, gave us the whole History of the *Black Prince;* concluding, that, in Sir *Richard Baker's* Opinion, *Edward* the Third was one of the greatest Princes that ever sat upon the *English* Throne.

We were thereupon shewn *Edward* the Confessor's Tomb; upon which Sir ROGER acquainted us, that he was the first who touched for the Evil; and afterwards *Henry* the Fourth's, upon which he shook his Head, and told us there was fine Reading in the Casualties of that Reign.

Our Conductor then pointed to that Monument where there is the Figure of one of our *English* Kings without an Head; and upon giving us to know, that the Head, which was of beaten Silver, had been stolen away several Years since: Some Whig, I'll warrant you, says Sir ROGER; you ought to lock up your Kings better; they will carry off the Body too, if you don't take care.

The glorious Names of *Henry* the Fifth and Queen *Elizabeth* gave the Knight great Opportunities of shining and of doing Justice to Sir *Richard Baker*, who, as our Knight observed with some Surprise, had a great many Kings in him, whose Monuments he had not seen in the Abbey.

For my own part, I could not but be pleased to see the Knight show such an honest Passion for the Glory of his Country, and such a respectful Gratitude to the Memory of its Princes. I must not omit, that the Benevolence of my good old Friend, which flows out towards every one he converses with, made him very kind to our Interpreter, whom he looked upon as an extraordinary Man; for which reason he shook him by the Hand at parting, telling him, that he should be very glad to see him at his Lodgings in *Norfolk-Buildings,* and talk over these Matters with him more at leisure.

Sir Roger at the Play

Chapter XXIII: Sir Roger at the Playhouse

*Respicere exemplar vitæ morumque jubebo
Doctum imitatorem, et veras hinc ducere voces.*

HORACE

MY Friend Sir ROGER DE COVERLEY, when we last met together at the Club, told me that he had a great Mind to see the new Tragedy with me, assuring me at the same time, that he had not been at a Play these twenty years. The last I saw, said Sir ROGER, was the *Committee*, which I should not have gone to neither, had not I been told before-hand that it was a good Church-of-*England* Comedy. He then proceeded to inquire of me who this distressed Mother was; and upon hearing that she was *Hector's* Widow, he told me that her Husband was a brave Man, and that when he was a School-boy, he had read his Life at the End of the Dictionary. My Friend asked me in the next place, if there would not be some danger in coming home late, in case the *Mohocks* should be abroad. I assure you, says he, I thought I had fallen into their Hands last Night; for I observed two or three lusty black Men that followed me half way up *Fleet-street*, and mended their pace behind me, in proportion as I put on to get away from them. You must know, continued the Knight with a

Smile, I fancied they had a mind to *hunt* me; for I remember an honest Gentleman in my Neighbourhood, who was served such a trick in King *Charles* the Second's time; for which reason he has not ventured himself in Town ever since. I might have shown them very good Sport, had this been their Design; for as I am an old Fox-hunter, I should have turned and dodged, and have played them a thousand Tricks they had never seen in their Lives before. Sir ROGER added, that if these Gentlemen had any such Intention, they did not succeed very well in it: for I threw them out, says he, at the End of *Norfolk-Street*, where I doubled the Corner and got Shelter in my Lodgings before they could imagine what was become of me. However, says the Knight, if Captain SENTRY will make one with us to-morrow night, and if you will both of you call upon me about four o'Clock, that we may be at the House before it is full, I will have my own Coach in readiness to attend you, for *John* tells me he has got both the Fore-Wheels mended.

The Captain, who did not fail to meet me there at the appointed Hour, bid Sir ROGER fear nothing, for that he had put on the same Sword which he made use of at the Battle of *Steenkirk*. Sir ROGER's Servants, and among the rest my old Friend the Butler, had, I found, provided themselves with good oaken Plants, to attend their Master upon this occasion. When we had placed him in his Coach, with

Sir Roger at the Playhouse

myself at his left-hand, the Captain before him, and his Butler at the Head of his Footmen in the Rear, we convoyed him in Safety to the Playhouse, where after having marched up the Entry in good order, the Captain and I went in with him, and seated him betwixt us in the Pit. As soon as the House was full, and the Candles lighted, my old Friend stood up and looked about him with that Pleasure, which a Mind seasoned with Humanity naturally feels in itself, at the sight of a Multitude of People who seem pleased with one another, and partake of the same common Entertainment. I could not but fancy to myself, as the old Man stood up in the middle of the Pit, that he made a very proper Centre to a tragick Audience. Upon the entring of *Pyrrhus*, the Knight told me that he did not believe the King of *France* himself had a better Strut. I was indeed very attentive to my old Friend's Remarks, because I looked upon them as a Piece of natural Criticism, and was well pleased to hear him, at the Conclusion of almost every Scene, telling me that he could not imagine how the Play would end. One while he appeared much concerned for *Andromache*; and a little while after as much for *Hermione*; and was extremely puzzled to think what would become of *Pyrrhus*.

When Sir ROGER saw *Andromache's* obstinate Refusal to her Lover's Importunities, he whispered me in the Ear, that he was sure she would never have him; to which he added, with a more than ordinary

Vehemence, you can't imagine, Sir, what 'tis to have to do with a Widow. Upon *Pyrrhus* his threatning afterwards to leave her, the Knight shook his Head and muttered to himself, Ay, do if you can. This Part dwelt so much upon my Friend's Imagination, that at the close of the Third Act, as I was thinking of something else, he whispered me in my Ear, These Widows, Sir, are the most perverse Creatures in the World. But pray, says he, you that are a Critick, is the Play according to your Dramatic Rules, as you call them? Should your People in Tragedy always talk to be understood? Why, there is not a single Sentence in this Play that I do not know the meaning of.

The Fourth Act very luckily begun before I had time to give the old Gentleman an Answer: Well, says the Knight, sitting down with great Satisfaction, I suppose we are now to see *Hector's* Ghost. He then renewed his Attention, and, from time to time, fell a praising the Widow. He made, indeed, a little Mistake as to one of her Pages, whom at his first entering he took for *Astyanax;* but quickly set himself right in that Particular, though, at the same time, he owned he should have been very glad to have seen the little Boy, who, says he, must needs be a very fine Child by the Account that is given of him. Upon *Hermione's* going off with a Menace to *Pyrrhus*, the Audience gave a loud Clap, to which Sir ROGER added, on my Word, a notable young Baggage!

As there was a very remarkable Silence and Stil-

Sir Roger at the Playhouse

ness in the Audience during the whole Action, it was natural for them to take the Opportunity of these Intervals between the Acts, to express their Opinion of the Players and of their respective Parts. Sir ROGER hearing a Cluster of them praise *Orestes*, struck in with them, and told them, that he thought his Friend *Pylades* was a very sensible Man; as they were afterwards applauding *Pyrrhus*, Sir ROGER put in a second time: And let me tell you, says he, though he speaks but little, I like the old Fellow in Whiskers as well as any of them. Captain SENTRY seeing two or three Wags, who sat near us, lean with an attentive Ear towards Sir ROGER, and fearing lest they should smoke the Knight, plucked him by the Elbow, and whispered something in his Ear, that lasted till the Opening of the fifth Act. The Knight was wonderfully attentive to the Account which *Orestes* gives of *Pyrrhus* his Death, and at the Conclusion of it, told me it was such a bloody Piece of Work, that he was glad it was not done upon the Stage. Seeing afterward *Orestes* in his raving Fit, he grew more than ordinary serious, and took occasion to moralize (in his way) upon an Evil Conscience, adding, that *Orestes, in his Madness, looked as if he saw something.*

As we were the first that came into the House, so we were the last that went out of it; being resolved to have a clear Passage for our old Friend, whom we did not care to venture among the justling of the

The Coverley Papers

Crowd. Sir ROGER went out fully satisfied with his Entertainment, and we guarded him to his Lodging in the same manner that we brought him to the Playhouse; being highly pleased, for my own part, not only with the Performance of the excellent Piece which had been presented, but with the Satisfaction which it had given to the old Man.

Chapter XXIV: Sir Roger at Vaux-Hall

Criminibus debent Hortos.
JUVENAL

AS I was sitting in my Chamber and thinking on a Subject for my next *Spectator*, I heard two or three irregular Bounces at my Landlady's Door, and upon the opening of it, a loud chearful Voice inquiring whether the Philosopher was at Home. The Child who went to the Door answered very innocently, that he did not lodge there. I immediately recollected that it was my good Friend Sir ROGER's Voice; and that I had promised to go with him on the Water to *Spring-Garden*, in case it proved a good Evening. The Knight put me in mind of my Promise from the bottom the Stair-Case, but told me that if I was speculating he would stay below till I had done. Upon my coming down, I found all the Children of the Family got about my old Friend, and my Landlady herself, who is a notable prating Gossip, engaged in a Conference with him; being mightily pleased with his stroking her little Boy upon the Head, and bidding him be a good Child, and mind his Book.

We were no sooner come to the *Temple*-Stairs, but we were surrounded with a Crowd of Watermen, offering us their respective Services. Sir ROGER after

The Coverley Papers

having looked about him very attentively, spied one with a Wooden-Leg, and immediately gave him Orders to get his Boat ready. As we were walking towards it, *You must know*, says Sir ROGER, *I never make use of any body to row me, that has not either lost a Leg or an Arm. I would rather bate him a few Strokes of his Oar than not employ an honest Man that has been wounded in the Queen's Service. If I was a Lord or a Bishop, and kept a Barge, I would not put a Fellow in my Livery that had not a Wooden Leg.* My old Friend, after having seated himself, and trimmed the Boat with his Coachman, who, being a very sober Man, always serves for Ballast on these Occasions, we made the best of our Way for *Vaux-Hall*. Sir ROGER obliged the Waterman to give us the History of his right Leg, and hearing that he had left it at *La Hogue*, with many Particulars which passed in that glorious Action, the Knight in the Triumph of his Heart made several Reflexions on the Greatness of the *British* Nation; as, that one *Englishman* could beat three *Frenchmen*; that we could never be in danger of Popery so long as we took care of our Fleet; that the *Thames* was the noblest River in *Europe*; that *London-Bridge* was a greater Piece of Work, than any of the seven Wonders of the World; with many other honest Prejudices which naturally cleave to the Heart of a true *Englishman*.

After some short Pause, the old Knight turning about his Head twice or thrice, to take a Survey of

Gordon Ross, del.

Sir Roger Reflects
that the Thames is the noblest River

Sir Roger at Vaux-Hall

this great Metropolis, bid me observe how thick the City was set with Churches, and that there was scarce a single Steeple on this side *Temple-Bar*. *A most Heathenish Sight!* says Sir ROGER: *There is no Religion at this End of the Town. The fifty new Churches will very much mend the Prospect; but Church-work is slow, Church-work is slow!*

I do not remember I have any where mentioned, in Sir ROGER's Character, his Custom of saluting every body that passes by him with a Good-morrow, or a Good-night. This the old Man does out of the overflowings of his Humanity, though at the same time it renders him so popular among all his Country Neighbours, that it is thought to have gone a good way in making him once or twice Knight of the Shire. He cannot forbear this Exercise of Benevolence even in Town, when he meets with any one in his morning or evening Walk. It broke from him to several Boats that passed by us upon the Water; but to the Knight's great Surprise, as he gave the Good-night to two or three young Fellows a little before our landing, one of them, instead of returning the Civility, asked us, what queer old Put we had in the Boat, with a great deal of the like *Thames*-Ribaldry. Sir ROGER seemed a little shocked at first, but at length assuming a Face of Magistracy, told us, *That if he were a* Middlesex *Justice, he would make such Vagrants know that her Majesty's subjects were no more to be abused by Water than by Land.* We were now arrived at *Spring-*

Garden, which is exquisitely pleasant at this time of the Year. When I considered the Fragrancy of the Walks and Bowers, with the Choirs of Birds that sung upon the Trees, and the loose Tribe of People that walked under their Shades, I could not but look upon the Place as a kind of *Mohometan* Paradise. Sir ROGER told me it put him in mind of a little Coppice by his House in the Country, which his Chaplain used to call an Aviary of Nightingales. *You must understand*, says the Knight, *there is nothing in the World that pleases a Man in Love so much as your Nightingale. Ah, Mr.* SPECTATOR! *the many Moonlight Nights that I have walked by myself, and thought on the Widow by the Musick of the Nightingale!* He here fetched a deep Sigh, and was falling into a Fit of musing, when a Mask, who came behind him, gave him a gentle Tap upon the Shoulder, and asked him if he would drink a Bottle of Mead with her? But the Knight being startled at so unexpected a Familiarity, and displeased to be interrupted in his Thoughts of the Widow, told her, *She was a wanton Baggage*, and bid her go about her Business.

We concluded our Walk with a Glass of *Burton*-Ale, and a Slice of Hung-Beef. When we had done eating, the Knight called a Waiter, and bid him carry the Remainder to the Waterman that had but one Leg. The Fellow stared at the oddness of the Message, and was going to be saucy; upon which I ratified the Knight's Commands with a peremptory Look.

Chapter XXV: Sir Roger, the Widow, Will Honeycomb, and Milton

Torva leæna lupum sequitur, lupus ipse capellam;
Florentem cytisum sequitur lasciva capella.

VIRGIL

AS we were at the Club last Night, I observed my Friend Sir ROGER, contrary to his usual Custom, sat very silent, and instead of minding what was said by the Company, was whistling to himself in a very thoughtful Mood, and playing with a Cork. I jogged Sir ANDREW FREEPORT who sat between us; and as we were both observing him, we saw the Knight shake his Head, and heard him say, to himself, *A foolish Woman! I can't believe it.* Sir ANDREW gave him a gentle pat upon the Shoulder, and offered to lay him a Bottle of Wine that he was thinking of the Widow. My old Friend started, and recovering out of his brown Study, told Sir ANDREW that once in his Life he had been in the right. In short, after some little Hesitation, Sir ROGER told us in the Fulness of his Heart that he had just received a Letter from his Steward, which acquainted him that his old Rival and Antagonist in the Country, Sir *David Dundrum*, had been making a Visit to the Widow. However, says Sir ROGER, I can never think that she'll have a Man that's half a Year older than I am, and a noted Republican into the Bargain.

Will Honeycomb, who looks upon Love as his particular Province, interrupting our Friend with a jaunty Laugh; I thought, Knight, says he, thou hadst lived long enough in the World, not to pin thy Happiness upon one that is a Woman and a Widow. I think that without Vanity I may pretend to know as much of the Female World as any Man in *Great Britain*, though the chief of my Knowledge consists in this, that they are not to be known. Will immediately, with his usual Fluency, rambled into an Account of his own Amours. I am now, says he, upon the Verge of Fifty, (though by the way we all knew he was turned of Threescore.) You may easily guess, continued Will, that I have not lived so long in the World without having had some Thoughts of *settling* in it, as the Phrase is. To tell you truly, I have several times tried my Fortune that way, though I can't much boast of my Success.

I made my first Addresses to a young Lady in the Country; but when I thought things were pretty well drawing to a Conclusion, her Father happening to hear that I had formerly boarded with a Surgeon, the old Put forbid me his House, and within a Fortnight after married his Daughter to a Fox-hunter in the Neighbourhood.

I made my next Application to a Widow, and attacked her so briskly, that I thought myself within

"She never saw a Gentleman
with such a Spindle Pair of legs as Mr. Honeycomb"

Sir Roger, the Widow, and Milton

a Fortnight of her. As I waited upon her one Morning, she told me, that she intended to keep her Ready Money and Jointure in her own Hand, and desired me to call upon her Attorney in *Lions-Inn*, who would adjust with me what it was proper for me to add to it. I was so rebuffed by this Overture, that I never inquired either for her or her Attorney afterwards.

A few Months after I addressed myself to a young Lady who was an only Daughter, and of a good Family: I danced with her at several Balls, squeezed her by the Hand, said soft things to her, and in short made no doubt of her Heart; and tho' my Fortune was not equal to hers, I was in hopes that her fond Father would not deny her the Man she had fixed her Affections upon. But as I went one Day to the House in order to break the matter to him, I found the whole Family in Confusion, and heard to my unspeakable Surprise, that Miss *Jenny* was that very Morning run away with the Butler.

I then courted a second Widow, and am at a loss to this Day how I came to miss her, for she had often commended my Person and Behaviour. Her Maid indeed told me one Day, that her Mistress had said she never saw a Gentleman with such a spindle Pair of Legs as Mr. HONEYCOMB.

After this I laid Siege to four Heiresses successively, and being a handsom young Dog in those Days, quickly made a Breach in their Hearts; but I don't know how it came to pass, though I seldom failed of getting the Daughters Consent, I could never in my Life get the old People on my side.

I could give you an Account of a thousand other unsuccessful Attempts, particularly of one which I made some Years since upon an old Woman, whom I had certainly born away with flying Colours, if her Relations had not come pouring in to her Assistance from all Parts of *England*; nay, I believe I should have got her at last, had not she been carried off by a hard Frost.

As WILL's Transitions are extremely quick, he turned from Sir ROGER, and applying himself to me, told me there was a Passage in the Book I had considered last *Saturday*, which deserved to be writ in Letters of Gold; and taking out a Pocket-*Milton*, read the following Lines, which are Part of one of *Adam's* Speeches to *Eve* after the Fall.

> *Oh! why did God,*
> *Creator wise! that peopled highest Heav'n*
> *With Spirits masculine, create at last*
> *This Novelty on Earth, this fair Defect*
> *Of Nature? and not fill the World at once*
> *With Men, as Angels, without Feminine?*
> *Or find some other way to generate*
> *Mankind? This Mischief had not then befall'n,*
> *And more that shall befall, innumerable*
> *Disturbances on Earth through Female Snares,*

Sir Roger, the Widow, and Milton

And strait Conjunction with this Sex: for either
He never shall find out fit Mate; but such
As some misfortune brings him, or mistake;
Or, whom he wishes most, shall seldom gain
Through her perverseness; but shall see her gain'd
By a far worse: or if she love, withheld
By Parents; or his happiest Choice too late
Shall meet already link'd, and Wedlock-bound
To a fell Adversary, his Hate or Shame;
Which infinite Calamity shall cause
To human Life, and Household Peace confound.

Sir ROGER listened to this Passage with great Attention, and desiring Mr. HONEYCOMB to fold down a Leaf at the Place, and lend him his Book, the Knight put it up in his Pocket, and told us that he would read over those Verses again before he went to Bed.

Chapter XXVI: Sir Roger Passeth Away

Heu Pietas! heu prisca Fides!
VIRGIL

WE last Night received a Piece of ill News at our Club, which very sensibly afflicted every one of us. I question not but my Readers themselves will be troubled at the hearing of it. To keep them no longer in suspense, Sir ROGER DE COVERLEY *is dead*. He departed this Life at his House in the Country, after a few Weeks Sickness. Sir ANDREW FREEPORT has a Letter from one of his Correspondents in those Parts, that informs him the old Man caught a Cold at the County-Sessions, as he was very warmly promoting an Address of his own penning, in which he succeeded according to his Wishes. But this Particular comes from a Whig Justice of Peace, who was always Sir ROGER's Enemy and Antagonist. I have Letters both from the Chaplain and Captain SENTREY which mention nothing of it, but are filled with many Particulars to the honour of the good old Man. I have likewise a Letter from the Butler, who took so much care of me last Summer when I was at the Knight's House. As my Friend the Butler mentions, in the Simplicity of his Heart, several Circumstances the others have passed over in Silence, I shall give my

Sir Roger Passeth Away

Reader a Copy of his Letter, without any Alteration or Diminution.

Honoured Sir,
'Knowing that you was my old Master's good
'Friend, I could not forbear sending you the melan-
'choly News of his Death, which has afflicted the
'whole Country, as well as his poor Servants, who
'loved him, I may say, better than we did our Lives.
'I am afraid he caught his Death the last County-
'Sessions, where he would go to see Justice done to
'a poor Widow Woman, and her Fatherless Children,
'that had been wronged by a neighbouring Gentle-
'man; for you know, Sir, my good Master was always
'the poor Man's Friend. Upon his coming home, the
'first Complaint he made was, that he had lost his
'Rost-Beef Stomach, not being able to touch a Sir-
'loin, which was served up according to custom; and
'you know he used to take great delight in it. From
'that time forward he grew worse and worse, but
'still kept a good Heart to the last. Indeed we were
'once in great hope of his Recovery, upon a kind
'Message that was sent him from the Widow Lady
'whom he had made love to the forty last Years of
'his Life; but this only proved a Lightning before
'Death. He has bequeathed to this Lady, as a token
'of his Love a great Pearl Necklace, and a Couple
'of Silver Bracelets set with Jewels, which belonged
'to my good old Lady his Mother: He has be-

'queathed the fine white Gelding, that he used to
'ride a hunting upon, to his Chaplain, because he
'thought he would be kind to him, and has left you
'all his Books. He has, moreover, bequeathed to the
'Chaplain a very pretty Tenement with good Lands
'about it. It being a very cold Day when he made his
'Will, he left for Mourning, to every Man in the
'Parish, a great Frize Coat, and to every Woman, a
'black Riding-hood. It was a most moving sight to
'see him take leave of his poor Servants, commend-
'ing us all for our Fidelity, whilst we were not able
'to speak a word for weeping. As we most of us are
'grown gray-headed in our dear Master's Service,
'he has left us Pensions and Legacies, which we may
'live very comfortly upon, the remaining part of our
'Days. He has bequeathed a great deal more in Char-
'ity, which is not yet come to my Knowledge, and it
'is peremptorily said in the Parish, that he has left
'Money to build a Steeple to the Church; for he was
'heard to say some time ago, that if he lived two
'Years longer, *Coverley* Church should have a Stee-
'ple to it. The Chaplain tells every Body that he
'made a very good End, and never speaks of him
'without Tears. He was buried according to his own
'Directions, among the Family of the COVERLIES,
'on the Left Hand of his Father Sir *Arthur*. The
'Coffin was carried by six of his Tenants, and the Pall
'held up by six of the *Quorum:* The whole Parish
'followed the Corps with heavy Hearts, and in their

Sir Roger Passeth Away

'Mourning Suits, the Men in Frize, and the Women
'in Riding Hoods. Captain SENTREY, my Master's
'Nephew, has taken possession of the Hall-House,
'and the whole Estate. When my old Master saw
'him a little before his Death, he shook him by the
'Hand, and wished him Joy of the Estate which was
'falling to him, desiring him only to make a good
'Use of it, and to pay the several Legacies, and the
'Gifts of Charity which he told him he had left as
'Quit-rents upon the Estate. The Captain truly seems
'a courteous Man, though he says but little. He
'makes much of those whom my Master loved, and
'shows great Kindnesses to the old House-dog, that
'you know my poor Master was so fond of. It would
'have gone to your Heart to have heard the Moans
'the dumb Creature made on the Day of my Master's
'Death. He has never joyed himself since; no more
'has any of us. 'Twas the melancholiest Day for the
'poor People that ever happened in *Worcestershire*.
'This is all from,

'*Honoured Sir*,
'*Your most sorrowful Servant*,
Edward Biscuit.

P. S. 'My Master desired, some Weeks before he
'died, that a Book which comes up to you by the Car-
'rier should be given to Sir ANDREW FREEPORT, in
'his Name.'

This Letter, notwithstanding the poor Butler's

The Coverley Papers

manner of writing it, gave us such an Idea of our good old Friend, that upon the reading of it there was not a dry Eye in the Club. Sir ANDREW opening the Book, found it to be a Collection of Acts of Parliament. There was in particular the Act of Uniformity, with some Passages in it marked by Sir ROGER's own Hand. Sir ANDREW found that they related to two or three Points, which he had disputed with Sir ROGER the last time he appeared at the Club. Sir ANDREW, who would have been merry at such an Incident on another Occasion, at the sight of the old Man's Hand-writing burst into Tears, and put the Book into his Pocket. Captain SENTREY informs us, that the Knight has left Rings and Mourning for every one in the Club.

Translations of the Mottoes

THE AUTHOR'S PREFACE. *Horace, Ars Poetica, 143:*
   One with a flash begins, and ends in smoke;
   Another out of smoke brings glorious light,
   And (without raising expectation high)
   Surprises us with dazzling miracles.—ROSCOMMON.

CHAPTER I. *Juvenal, Satires, vii. 167:*
   Six more, at least, join their consenting voice.

CHAPTER II. *Horace, I Odes, xvii. 14:*
   Here plenty's liberal horn shall pour
   Of fruits for thee a copious show'r,
   Rich honours of the quiet plain.

CHAPTER III. *Phaedre, Epilogues, I. 2:*
   The Athenians erected a large statue to Aesop, and placed him, though a slave, on a lasting pedestal: to show that the way to honour lies open indifferently to all.

CHAPTER IV. *Phaedre, Fables, v. 2:*
   Out of breath to no purpose, and very busy about nothing.

CHAPTER V. *Horace, Satires, ii. 3:*
   Of plain good sense, untutor'd in the schools.

CHAPTER VI. *Virgil, Aeneid, ii. 755:*
   All things are full of horror and affright,
   And dreadful ev'n the silence of the night.
                                             —DRYDEN.

CHAPTER VII. *Pythagoras:*
   First, in obedience to thy country's rites,
   Worship th' immortal gods.

CHAPTER VIII. *Virgil, Aeneid, iv. 4:*
   Her looks were deep imprinted in his heart.

Translations of the Mottoes

CHAPTER IX. *Horace, I Epistles, xviii. 24:*
    .... The dread of nothing more
Than to be thought necessitous and poor.—POOLY.

CHAPTER X. *Juvenal, Satires, x. 356:*
    Pray for a sound mind in a sound body.

CHAPTER XI. *Virgil, Eclogues, viii. 108:*
    With voluntary dreams they cheat their minds.

CHAPTER XII. *Virgil, Aeneid, iv. 73:*
    .... The fatal dart
Sticks in his side, and rankles in his heart.—DRYDEN.

CHAPTER XIII. *Virgil, Eclogues, i. 20:*
    The city men call Rome, unskilful clown,
I thought resembled this our humble town.
                      —WHARTON.

CHAPTER XIV. *Virgil, Georgics, i. 415:*
    .... I deem their breasts inspired
With a divine sagacity. ....

CHAPTER XV. *Publius Syrius, Fragment:*
    An agreeable companion upon the road is as good as a coach.

CHAPTER XVI. *Horace, 4 Odes, iv. 33:*
    Yet the best blood by learning is refined,
And virtue arms the solid mind;
Whilst vice will stain the noblest race,
And the paternal stamp efface.—OLDISWORTH.

CHAPTER XVII. *Virgil, Aeneid, vi. 832:*
    This thirst of kindred blood, my sons, detest,
Nor turn your force against your country's breast.
                      —DRYDEN.

Translations of the Mottoes

Chapter XVIII. *Virgil, Aeneid, vii. 748:*
    A plundering race, still eager to invade,
    On spoil they live, and make of theft a trade.

Chapter XIX. *Virgil, Eclogues, x. 63:*
    Once more, ye woods, adieu.

Chapter XX. *Tullius:*
    That man may be called impertinent, who considers not the circumstances of time, or engrosses the conversation, or makes himself the subject of his discourse, or pays no regard to the company he is in.

Chapter XXI. *Ovid, Ars Amatoris, i. 241:*
    Most rare is now our old simplicity.—DRYDEN.

Chapter XXII. *Horace, I. Epistles, vi. 27:*
    With Ancus, and with Numa, kings of Rome,
    We must descend into the silent tomb.

Chapter XXIII. *Horace, Ars Poetica, 327:*
    Keep Nature's great original in view,
    And thence the living images pursue.—FRANCIS.

Chapter XXIV. *Juvenal, Satires, i. 75:*
    A beauteous garden, but by vice maintain'd.

Chapter XXV. *Virgil, Eclogues, ii. 63:*
    Lions the wolves, and wolves the kids pursue,
    The kids sweet thyme,—and still I follow you.
                     —WHARTON.

Chapter XXVI. *Virgil, Aeneid, vi. 878:*
    Mirror of ancient faith!
    Undaunted worth! Inviolable truth!—DRYDEN.

SOME NOTES

"*To Give the Reader an Enjoyment of Allusions to Past Manners & Events*"

The Author's Preface. Page 1.
From the *Spectator*, No. 1, dated March 1, 1711-12. By Addison.

Page 5. *I made a Voyage to Grand Cairo, on purpose to take Measure of the Pyramid.* A half century's contention respecting the exact admeasurement of the Great Pyramid of Gizeh was a fair subject for ridicule in spite of Dr. Percy's stigma that the satire was "reprehensible." Mr. John Greaves originated the argument so long before the publication of this harmless raillery as 1646, in his Work entitled "Pyramidologia," and it seems to have been carried on with burning zeal and wonderful learning to the days of the *Spectator*, although death had removed Greaves from the discussion in 1652. In No. 7 the *Spectator* says, "I design to visit the next masquerade in the same Habit I wore at Grand Cairo."

Page 5. THE COFFEE HOUSES. *There is no Place of general Resort wherein I do not make my Appearance.* The chief places of resort were coffee and chocolate houses, in which some men almost lived, insomuch that whoever wished to find a gentleman commonly asked, not where he resided, but which coffee house he frequented? No decently attired idler was excluded, provided he laid down his penny at the bar; but which he could seldom do without struggling through the crowd of beaux who fluttered round the lovely bar-maid. Here the proud nobleman or country squire were not to be distinguished from the genteel thief and daring highwayman. "Pray Sir," says Aimwell to Gibbet, in Farquhar's *Beaux Stratagem*, "han't I seen your face at *Will's* coffee house?" The robber's reply is:—"Yes, Sir; and at *White's* too."

Coffee houses, from the time of their commencement in 1652, served instead of newspapers:—they were *arenæ* for political discussion. Journalism was then in its infancy: the first daily newspaper (*The Daily Courant*) was scarcely two years old, and was too small to contain much news; as were the other journals then extant. Hence the fiercely contested polemics of the period were either waged in single pamphlets or in periodicals started to advocate or to oppose some particular question, and laid down when that was settled. The peaceful leading article and mild letter "to the Editor" had not come into vogue as safety valves for the escape of overboiling party zeal; and the hot blood, roused in public rooms to quarrelling pitch, was too often cooled by the rapier's point.

Each coffee house had its political or literary specialty; and of those enumerated in the present paper, WILL's was the rendezvous for the wits and poets. It was named after William Urwin, its proprietor, and was situated at No. 1, Bow Street, at the corner of Great Russell Street, Covent Garden; the coffee-room was on the first floor, the lower part having been occupied as a retail shop. Dryden's patronage and frequent appearance made the reputation of the house, which was afterwards maintained by other celebrated characters. De Foe wrote—about the year 1720—that "after the play the best company go to *Tom's* or *Will's* Coffee house near adjoining; where there is playing picquet and the best conversation till midnight. Here you will see blue and green ribbons and stars familiarly, and talking with the same freedom, as if they had left their quality and degrees of distance at home." The turn of conversation is happily hit off in the *Spectator* for June 12th, 1712, when a false report of the death of Louis XIV. had reached England:—"Upon my going into *Will's* I found their discourse was gone off from the death of the *French* king to that of Monsieur *Boileau, Racine, Corneille*, and several other poets, whom they regretted on this occasion, as persons who would have obliged the world with very noble elegies on the death of so great a prince, and so eminent a patron of learning." It was from *Will's* coffee house that the *Tatler* dated his poetry.

The Coverley Papers

CHILD'S was in St. Paul's Churchyard. Its vicinity to the Cathedral and Doctor's Commons, made it the resort of the clergy and other ecclesiastical loungers. In one respect Child's was superseded by the *Chapter* in Paternoster Row.

THE ST. JAMES'S was the *Spectator's* head-quarters. It stood at the end of Pall Mall—of which it commanded a perspective view—near to, if not upon the site of what is now No. 87, St. James's Street, and close to *Ozinda's* chocolate house. These were the great party rallying places: "a Whig," says De Foe, "would no more go to the *Cocoa Tree* or *Ozinda's* than a Tory would be seen at *St. James's*." Swift, however, frequented the latter during his sojourn in London, 1710-13; till, fighting in the van of the Tory ranks, he could no longer show face there, and was obliged to relinquish the society of those literary friends whom, though Whigs, he cherished. Up to that time all his letters were addressed to the *St. James's* coffee house, and those from Mrs. Johnston (Stella) were enclosed under cover to Addison. Elliot, who kept the house, acted confidentially for his customers as a party agent; and was on occasions placed on a friendly footing with some of his distinguished guests. In Swift's Journal to Stella, under the date of Nov. 19, 1710, we find the following entry:—"This evening I christened our coffee-man Elliot's child; when the rogue had a most noble supper, and Steele and I sat amongst some scurvy company over a bowl of punch." This must have included some of Elliot's more intimate or private friends; for he numbered amongst his customers nearly all the Whig aristocracy. The *Tatler* (who dated his politics from the *St. James's*) enumerating the charges he was at to entertain his readers, assures them that "a good observer cannot even speak with Kidney ['keeper of the book debts of the outlying customers, and observer of all those who go off without paying,'] without clean linen."

The *Spectator*, in his 403rd number, gives a graphic picture of the company in the coffee-room:—"I first of all called in at *St. James's*, where I found the whole outward room in a buzz of politics. The speculations were but very indifferent towards the door, but grew finer as you advanced to the upper end of the room, and were so very much improved by a knot of theorists, who sat in the inner room, within the steams of the coffee-pot, that

Some Notes, &c.

I there heard the whole Spanish monarchy disposed of, and all the line of Bourbon provided for, in less than a quarter of an hour."

THE GRECIAN in Devereux Court derived its name from a Greek named Constantine, who introduced a new and improved method of making coffee, from the land of Epicurus. Perhaps from this cause, or from having set up his apparatus close to the Temple, he drew the Learned to his rooms. "All accounts of Learning," saith the *Tatler*, "shall be under the Title of the *Grecian*." The alumni appear to have disputed at a particular table. "I cannot keep an ingenious Man," continues Bickerstaff, "to go daily to the *Grecian* without allowing him some plain Spanish to be as able as others at the learned Table." The glory of the *Grecian* outlasted that of the rest, and it remained a tavern till 1843.

JONATHAN'S, in Change Alley, the general mart for stock-jobbers, was the precursor of the present Stock Exchange in Capel Court. The hero of Mrs. Centlivre's comedy "A Bold Stroke for a Wife," performs at *Jonathan's* his most successful deception on the city guardian of his mistress.

The other coffee houses will be noticed as they occur in the text.

Page 7. *It is laid and concerted (as all other Matters of Importance are) in a Club.* The word Club as applied to convivial meetings, is derived from the Saxon *cleafan*, to divide, "because," says Skinner, "the expenses are divided into shares or portions."

Clubs were more general in the days of the *Spectator* than perhaps at any other period of our history. Throughout the previous half-century public discord had dissevered private society; and, at the Restoration, men yearned for fellowship; but as, even yet, political danger lurked under an unguarded expression or a rash toast, companions could not be too carefully chosen. Persons therefore whose political opinions and private tastes coincided, made a practice of meeting in clubs. This principle of congeniality took all manner of odd turns, but the political clubs of the time played an important part in history.

The idea of uniting the authors of a periodical in a club—though an obvious one—was calculated to bring out sparkling contrasts of character. But it was not successfully elaborated. Each personage was greatly dissociated from the club in future papers. Hence the faults some critics have found with the character of Sir ROGER; for, taken in connection with the society, it has not the coherence it would have had, if the club scheme had been efficiently developed. But viewed separately, what—as the reader of these pages will own—can be more harmonious or natural?

The eccentric clubs were fruitful sources of satire to the *Spectator*. He is merry on the *Mummers'*, the *Two-penny*, the *Ugly*, the *Fighting*, the *Fringe-Glove*, the *Hum-drum*, the *Doldrum*, the *Everlasting*, and the *Lovers'* clubs; on clubs of fat men, of tall men, of one-eyed men, and of men who lived in the same street. This last was a social arrangement almost necessary at a time when distant visits were impossible at night, not only from the bad condition of the streets, but from the ravages of the dastardly "Mohock Club," of which hereafter.

Page 7. *Those who have a mind to correspond with me may direct their Letters to the Spectator at Mr. Buckley's.*

"This day is published
A paper entitled THE SPECTATOR, which will be continued every day. Printed for Sam. Buckley at the Dolphin, in Little Britain, and sold by A. Baldwin, in Warwick Lane."
Daily Courant, March 1st, 1711.

The above names form the imprint to the *Spectator's* early papers. From No. 18 appears, in addition, "Charles Lillie [perfumer, bookseller and secretary to the *Tatler's* "Court of Honour"] at the corner of Beaufort buildings in the Strand." From the date, August 5th, 1712, (No. 449) Jacob Tonson's imprint is appended. About that time he removed from Gray's Inn Gate to "the Strand, over against Catherine Street."

Samuel Buckley had eventually an innocent hand in the discontinuance of the *Spectator*. He was the "writer and printer" of the first daily newspaper—*The Daily Courant*, and having published on the 7th of April, 1712, a memorial of the States General reflecting on the English government, he was brought in custody to the

Some Notes, &c.

bar of the House of Commons. The upshot was some strong resolutions respecting the licentiousness of the press (which had indeed been commented on at the opening of parliament in the Queen's Speech) and the imposition of the halfpenny stamp on periodicals. To this addition to the price of the *Spectator* is attributed its downfall.

Chapter I: Sir Roger and the Club
No. 2. Friday, March 2, 1711-12. By Steele.

Page 9. *The first of our Society is a Gentleman of Worcestershire of ancient Descent, a Baronet, his Name is Sir* ROGER DE COVERLEY. Whenever any striking individuality appears in print, the public love to suppose that, instead of being the embodied representative of a class, it is an actual portrait. A thousand conjectures were afloat as to the original of Sir ROGER DE COVERLEY, at the time and long after the *Spectator's* papers were in current circulation. These were revived by a passage in the preface to Budgell's *Theophrastus* in which he asserted in general terms that most of the characters in the *Spectator* were conspicuously known. It was not however till 1783, when Tyers named Sir John Packington of Westwood, Worcestershire, that any prototype to Sir ROGER was definitely pointed out.

Tyer's assertion is not tenable. Except that Sir ROGER and Sir John were both baronets and lived in Worcestershire, each presents few points of similitude to the other:—Sir ROGER was a disappointed bachelor; Sir John was twice married: Sir ROGER, although more than once returned knight of the shire, was not an ardent politician; Sir John was, and sate for his native county in every parliament save one from his majority till his death. Westwood House—"in the middle of a wood that is cut into twelve large ridings; the whole encompassed with a park of six or seven miles,"—bears no greater resemblance to the description of Coverley Hall than the scores of Country houses which have wood about them. Sir ROGER is neither litigant nor lawyer, despite the universal applause bestowed by the Quarter session on his exposition of "a passage in the game-act:" Sir John was a barrister, and besides having been Recorder for the city of Worcester, proved himself so powerful a plaintiff that he ousted the then Bishop of

Worcester from his place of Royal Almoner for interfering in the County election.

The account of the *Spectator* and each member of his club was most likely fictitious; for the *Tatler* having been betrayed into personalities gave such grave offence, that Steele determined not to fall again into a like error. Had indeed the originals of Sir ROGER and his club-companions existed among, as Budgell asserts, the "conspicuous" characters of the day, literary history would assuredly have revealed them. But a better witness than Budgell testifies to the reverse. The *Spectator* emphatically disclaims personality in various passages:—In 262 he says "When I place an imaginary Name at the Head of a Character, I examine every Syllable, every Letter of it, that it may not bear any resemblance to one that is Real:" in another place,—"I would not make myself merry with a Piece of Pasteboard that is invested with a Public Character."

Page 9. *His Great Grandfather was Inventor of that famous Country-Dance called after him.* The real sponsor to the joyous conclusion of every ball has only been recently revealed after the most vigilant research. An autograph account by Ralph Thoresby, of the family of Calverley of Calverley in Yorkshire, dated 1717, and which is now in the possession of Sir W. Calverley Trevelyan, states that the tune of *Roger a Calverley* was named after Sir Roger of Calverley, who lived in the time of Richard the First. This Knight, according to the custom of that period, kept minstrels, who took the name from their office of *harper*. Their descendants possessed lands in the neighbourhood of *Calverley*, called *Harpersroids* and *Harper's Spring*. "The seal of this Sir Roger, appended to one of his charters, is large, with a chevalier on horseback."

The earliest printed copy of the tune which has yet been traced is in "a choice collection to a ground for a treble violin," by J. Playford, 1685. It appears again in 1695 in H. Playford's "Dancing Master." Mr. Chappell, author of the elaborate work on English Melodies, believes it to have been a hornpipe. That it was popular about the *Spectator's* time is shown from a passage in a Satirical history of Powel the Puppet man (1715):—"Upon the preludes being ended each party fell to bawling and calling for particular tunes. The hobnailed fellows, whose breeches and lungs seemed to be of the same leather, cry'd out for "Cheshire Rounds," "*Roger of Coverley*," "Joan's placket," and "Northern Nancy.""

Steele owned that the notion of adapting the name to the good genial old knight, originated with Swift.

Page 9. *When in Town he lives in Soho Square.* Sir ROGER had doubtless chosen this fashionable locality in the "fine gentleman" era of his career. We shall presently see, that on his subsequent visits to Town he changed his lodgings to humbler neighbourhoods. The splendour of Soho Square was only dawning, when Foreign Princes were taken to see Bloomsbury Square as one of the wonders of England. In 1681, the former had no more than eight residences in it, and the palace of the unfortunate Dukes of Monmouth filled up the entire South side. During Sir ROGER's supposed residence in Soho (then also called King's) Square he had for a neighbour Bishop Burnet. Only a few years later it lost caste; for by 1717 we find from Walpole's Anecdotes of Painting that Monmouth House had been converted into Auction Rooms.

Sir ROGER changed his residence at each subsequent visit to London. The *Spectator* in his 335th Number lodges him in Norfolk Street, Strand, and in No. 410 in Bow Street, Covent Garden.

Page 10. *Kicked Bully Dawson.* Dawson was a swaggering gentleman about Town, when Etheridge and Rochester were in full vogue. One of the Manuscript notes, by Oldys, upon the margins of the copy of Langbaine's account of the English Dramatic Poets, in the British Museum, mentions him thus:—

"The character of Captain Hackman in this Comedy [Shadwell's 'Squire of Alsatia'] was drawn as I have been told by old John Bowman the player, to expose Bully Dawson, a noted sharper, swaggerer, and debauchee about Town, especially in Blackfriars and its infamous purlieus."

Page 12. *He has his Shoes rubbed and his Periwig powdered at the Barber's as you go into the Rose.* The Rose stood at the end of a passage in Russell Street, adjoining the theatre which then, be it remembered, faced Drury Lane. It was here that on the 12th November 1712, the seconds on either side arranged the duel fought the next day by the Duke of Hamilton and Lord Mohun, in which both were killed.

Page 12. *Sir Andrew Freeport*. "To Sir ROGER who as a country gentleman appears to be a Tory; or, as it is generally expressed, an adherent to the landed interest, is opposed Sir ANDREW FREEPORT, a new man and a wealthy merchant, zealous for the money'd interest, and a Whig. Of this contrariety of opinions more consequences were at first intended than could be produced when the resolution was taken to exclude party from the paper." *Dr. Johnson's Life of Addison.*

No one has ventured to name originals either for the Templar or Sir Andrew Freeport.

Page 13. *Captain Sentry*. This character, heir to Sir ROGER, is said—with no more probability than attaches to the imagined origin of the others—to have been copied from Col. Kempenfeldt, father of the Admiral who was drowned in the *Royal George* when it went down at Spithead in 1782. The conjecture probably had no other foundation—a very frail one—than a eulogium on the colonel's character in Captain SENTRY's letter to the club announcing his induction into Sir ROGER's estate, and which forms the last of the Coverley papers.

Page 14. WILL HONEYCOMB. Col. Cleland of the Life Guards has been named as the real person here described: but as in the former instances the supposition is ill supported.

Chapter II: Coverley Hall

No. 106. Monday, July 2, 1711. By Addison.

Page 20. *He was afraid of being insulted with Latin and Greek at his own Table*. The literary acquirements of the Squirearchy of Sir ROGER's era were few. At a time not long antecedent, "an esquire passed for a great scholar if Hudibras, and Baker's Chronicle, Tarleton's Jests, and the Seven Champions of Christendom lay in his hall window among angling rods and fishing lines." But that Sir ROGER may appear in this, as in other respects, above the average of his order, there is in Coverley Hall a library rich in "divinity and MS. household receipts." Sir ROGER too had drawn many observations together out of his reading in

Some Notes, &c.

Baker's Chronicle, and other authors "who always lie in his Hall window;" and, however limited his own classic lore, it is certain that both in love and in friendship he displayed strong literary sympathies.

The perverse Widow whose cruelty so often darkened his whole existence, was a "reading lady," a "desperate scholar," and in argument "as learned as the best philosopher in Europe." One who, when in the country, "does not run into dairies, but reads upon the nature of plants—has a glass hive and comes into the garden out of books to see them work." In his friendship again, Sir ROGER was all for learning. Besides the *Spectator*,—to whom he eventually bequeathed his books—he indulged a Platonic admiration for Leonora, a Widow, formerly a celebrated beauty, and still a very lovely woman—who "turned all the passion of her sex into a love of books and retirement."

Chapter III: The Coverley Household
No. 107. Tuesday, July 3, 1711. By Steele.

Page 22. *The general Corruption of Manners in Servants is owing to the Conduct of Masters.* The account of Sir ROGER's domestics, in which his benevolence is made so vividly to beam forth, was "intended as a gentle admonition to thankless masters," whose harshness and brutality were not exaggerated in the fictions and plays of the time. It was quite usual for gentlemen to cane offending footmen, and to assail female servants with the coarsest abuse. On the other side, dependants took their revenge to the fullest extent;—sometimes by subtle artifice, at others by reckless dissipation and bold dishonesty. Newspapers, and criminal records, prove that Dean Swift's "Directions to Servants" was not an imaginative satire; but that every word was founded on fact. Indeed some of the experiences from which it was drawn were manifestly derived from his own drinking, cheating, and cringing man, Patrick. In the 88th number of the *Spectator*, Philo-Britannicus complains that although there is no place wherein servants labour less than in England, yet they are nowhere "so little respectful, more wasteful, more negligent, or where they so frequently change masters."

The Coverley Papers

That most of the vices of servants were due to the ill-conduct of masters—which the example of Sir ROGER in this Chapter is meant in all kindliness to expose and correct—the *Spectator* points out in many pages; but, especially, in his commentary on the letter of Philo-Britannicus. "All dependants," he observes, "run in some measure into the Measures and Behaviour of those whom they serve"—a fact which he humorously illustrates thus:—

"Falling in the other day at a victualling-house near the House of Peers, I heard the maid come down and tell the landlady at the bar, that my Lord Bishop swore he would throw her out at window if she did not bring up more mild beer, and that my Lord Duke would have a double mug of purl. My surprise was increased in hearing loud and rustic voices speak and answer to each other upon the public affairs by the names of the most illustrious of our nobility; till of a sudden one came running in, and cried the House was rising. Down came all the company together, and away: The ale-house was immediately filled with clamour, and scoring one mug to the Marquis of such a place, oil and vinegar to such an Earl, three quarts to my new Lord for wetting his title, and so forth. It is a thing too notorious to mention the crowds of servants, and their insolence, near the courts of justice, and the stairs towards the supreme assembly, where there is an universal mockery of all order, such riotous clamour and licentious confusion, that one would think the whole nation lived in jest, and there were no such thing as rule and distinction among us."

No. 96 of the *Spectator* and No. 87 of the *Guardian* are filled with the same subject. The short sketch, which ends the latter paper, of Lycurgus, "the Banker, the Council, and Parent of all his numerous Dependants," is a miniature copy of Sir ROGER by the same artist.

Various attempts were made to reform domestics; and among them we find, in the first issue of the *Spectator*, (No. 224) the advertisement of a society for the encouragement of good servants "at the office in Ironmonger Lane. The method," continues the advertisement, "has hitherto had very good effects, the benefits not being receivable without dutiful behaviour of the servants and a good character from their master."

Some Notes, &c.

Chapter IV: The Coverley Guest
No. 108. Wednesday, July 4, 1711. By Addison.

Page 28. WILL WIMBLE *is the younger Brother to a Baronet and descendant of the ancient Family of the Wimbles*. This delineation, like the rest of the *Spectator's* prominent characters, is too like life to have escaped the imputation of having been drawn from it. The received story is, that WILL WIMBLE was a Mr. Thomas Morecraft, younger son of a Yorkshire baronet. Steele knew this gentleman in early life and introduced him to Addison, by whose bounty he was for some time supported; for, though excelling in such small and profitless arts as are attributed to WILL WIMBLE, he had not the ingenuity to gain his own livelihood. When Addison died, Mr. Morecraft went to Ireland to his friend the Bishop of Kildare, at whose house in Fifth Street, Dublin, he died in 1741.

The attentive reader of the *Tatler* will find in it the germ of many of the characters in the *Spectator*—an additional argument against their having been drawn from actual individuals. The honourable Mr. Thomas Gules, who indicted Peter Plum in the Court of Honour for taking the wall of him, (*Tatler*, No. 256) will at once be recognized as the prototype of WILL WIMBLE. "The prosecutor alleged that he was the Cadet of a very ancient family; and that according to the principles of all the younger brothers of the said family, he had never sullied himself with business; but had chosen rather to starve like a man of honour, than do anything beneath his quality. He produced several witnesses that he had never employed himself beyond the twisting of a whip, or the making of a pair of nutcrackers, in which he only worked for his diversion, in order to make a present now and then to his friends."

Chapter V: The Coverley Lineage
No. 109. Thursday, July 5, 1711. By Steele.

Page 33. *He was the last Man that won a Prize in the Tilt Yard.* * * * *I do not know but it might be exactly where the Coffee House is now.*

"South from Charing Cross, on the right hand, in Stow's time, were divers handsome houses lately built before the park; then a large tilt yard for noblemen and others to exercise themselves in justing, turneying, and fighting at the barriers." One of these "handsome houses" afterwards became Jenny Man's "Tilt Yard Coffee House" in Whitehall, upon the site now occupied by the Paymaster General's office. It was the resort of military officers, until supplanted by Slaughter's in St. Martin's Lane. The *Spectator* states elsewhere that the mock military also frequented the Tilt Yard Coffee House—fellows who figured in laced hats, black cockades, and scarlet suits, and who manfully pulled the noses of quiet citizens who wore not swords.

Page 34. *Whereas the Ladies now walk as if they were in a Go-Cart.* The hooped petticoat was revived, not long before the date of this paper, by a mantua-maker named Selby. Against it keen war was waged in the *Spectator*. No. 127 is wholly devoted to the subject; Sir ROGER being incidentally enlisted as an ally.

It hath ever been considered a foible of the fair sex to run into extremes; and, while the promenade costume of that day (and indeed of scores of succeeding years) was more ample than the present crowded state of population would allow, the equestrian habit appears to have been tightened into a close imitation of male habiliments.—"I remember when I was at my friend Sir ROGER DE COVERLEY's," says the *Spectator*, (July 18, 1712) "about this time twelvemonth, an equestrian lady of this order appeared upon the plains which lie at a distance from his house. I was at that time walking in the fields with my old friend; and as his tenants ran out on every side to see so strange a sight, Sir ROGER asked one of them who came by us what it was? To which the country fellow replied, 'Tis a gentlewoman, saving your worship's presence, in a coat and hat. This produced a great deal of mirth at the knight's house, where we had a story at the same time of another of his tenants, who meeting this gentleman-like lady on the highway, was asked by her *whether that was* Coverley-Hall, the honest man seeing only the male part of the querist, replied, *Yes, Sir;* but upon the second question, *whether* Sir ROGER DE COVERLEY *was a married man*, having dropped his eye upon the petticoat, he changed his notes into *No, Madam*."

Some Notes, &c.

Chapter VI: The Coverley Ghost
No. 110. Friday, July 6, 1711. By Addison.

Page 38. *Feedeth the young Ravens that call upon Him.* "Who giveth fodder unto the cattle; and feedeth the young ravens that call upon Him."—*Psalm* cxlvii. 9.

Page 39. *Mr. Locke, in his Chapter of the Association of Ideas.*—Essay on Human Understanding, Book ii. chap. 33, section 10.

Chapter VII: The Coverley Sabbath
No. 112. Monday, July 9, 1711. By Addison.

Page 44. *As soon as the Sermon is finished, nobody presumes to stir till* Sir ROGER *is gone out of the Church.* The church close to which Addison was born, and where his father ministered, may have supplied some of the traits to the exquisite picture of a rural Sabbath which this chapter presents.

The parish church of Milston is a modest edifice, situated in a combe or hollow of the Wiltshire downs, about two miles north-west of Amesbury. In the parsonage house—now an honoured ruin—on the 1st of May, 1672, Joseph Addison was born. It is only separated from the grave-yard by a hawthorn fence, and must have been, when inhabited, the beau ideal of a country parsonage. It has a spacious garden, rich glebe, and commands a pretty view, bounded by the hill on which stands the church of Durrington.

Milston church remains nearly in the same state, as, during the first twelve years of his life which Addison passed under its shadow. As no benevolent parishioner took the hint conveyed in Sir ROGER's will, it is still without tower or steeple; the belfry being nothing more than a small louvered shed. Within, the church is partitioned off by tall worm-eaten pews, and is scarcely capable of holding a hundred persons. At the east end stands the communion table, "railed in." It was once lighted by a stained glass window; but of this it was deprived by the cupidity of a deceased incumbent. The same person was guilty of a worse act: —To oblige a friend—"a collector"—he actually tore out the leaf of the parish register which contained the entry of Joseph Addison's birth.

Milston church does not display the texts of Scripture attributed to the Coverley edifice. If any existed when Addison wrote, they must have been since effaced by white-wash.

Chapter VIII: Sir Roger in Love
No. 113. Tuesday, July 10, 1711. By Steele.

Page 53. *The Widow is the secret Cause of all that Inconsistency which appears in some Parts of my Friend's Discourse.* The notion that the perverse widow had a living, charming, provoking, original, has been more prevalent and better supported than that respecting any of the rest of the Coverley characters. Although a mere outline,—hinted rather than delineated amidst the picturesque group of last century figures—she is so suggestively shadowed forth that the reader himself insensibly vivifies the outline, feels her ascendency and doubles his pity for her kind-hearted victim. "The dignity of her aspect, the composure of her motion," and the polish of her repartee—heightened by the foil of her spiteful confidant—make us participate in Sir ROGER's awe; and, while we sympathize with his ardent admiration we tremble for the hapless presumption that aspires to "the finest Hand of any Woman in the World."—Her subtlety was unbounded. No coquette commands success who, besides varied resources, cannot ply her heart with the chastest dexterity; and the Widow's omnipotence was attained less by her personal charms and mental graces, than by the delicacy of her lures and the nice discrimination with which they were spread.

These faint but variegated tints are so truthfully blended in the Widow, that not only general readers, but acute critics have believed, that nothing short of the minutest experience of an equally desperate suit to an equally coy and fascinating original, could have inspired and executed the likeness. Both Addison and Steele had suffered from perverse Widows; and who knows but this "confluence of congenial sentiment" springing from a like source was one cause of these differently constituted men being long united in friendship?

Some Notes, &c.

The tantalising dominion under which Addison suffered when the Coverley papers were in progress, was exercised by the Countess Dowager of Warwick, whom he was anxiously courting; "perhaps," says Dr. Johnson, "with behaviour not very unlike that of Sir ROGER to his disdainful widow." The result, though different, was not happier than Sir ROGER's destiny. Not till four years after the Coverley papers had been finished did Addison succeed in his suit. "On the 2nd August, 1716," continues the biographer of the poets, "he married the Countess, on terms much like those on which a Turkish Princess is espoused; to whom the Sultan is reported to pronounce 'Daughter, I give thee this man for thy slave!'" This marriage was only a change from one sort of unhappiness to another,—from the intermittent vexations of a slighted lover, to the chronic miseries of an ill-matched husband.

Probability however rejects Lady Warwick as the model we seek. To find it we must, it is said, turn to Steele's tormentress. Addison's sufferings were in full force when the sketch was made; Steele's were past. Addison's tortures were too real and operative for the unchecked flow of that genial humour—for that fine tolerance of the Widow's cruelty—which pervades every allusion to her: Steele's pains had, on the contrary, been first assuaged by time and then, let us hope, extinguished by matrimony with another—and another. While therefore experience had made him master of a Widow's arts, the retrospect of what he had suffered from them was too remote to darken the shadows, or to sour the expression of the portrait. Hence it is his signature that appears to this paper, and his Widow who is said to have inspired them.

The information on which this belief is grounded is derived from Chalmers through Archdeacon Nares, to whom it was communicated by the Rev. Duke Yonge of Plympton in Devonshire. "My attention," says the reverend gentleman, "was first drawn to this subject by a very vague tradition in the family of Sir Thomas Crawley Boevey, of Flaxley Abbey in Gloucestershire, that Mrs. Catherine Boevey, widow of William Boevey, Esq., and who died January 21, 1726, was the original from whence the picture of the perverse widow in the *Spectator* was drawn. She was left a widow at the early age of 22, and by her portrait (now at Flaxley Abbey and drawn at a more advanced period of her life) appears to have been a woman of a handsome, dignified figure, as she is described to have been in the 113th No. of the *Spectator*. She was a personage well known and much distinguished in her day, and is described very respectably in the New Atalantis, under the name of Portia. From these facts I was induced to examine whether any internal evidence could be traced in the *Spectator* to justify the tradition. The result of that enquiry is as follows:—

"The papers in the *Spectator* which give the description of the widow, were certainly written by Steele, and that Mrs. Boevey was well known to Steele, and held by him in high estimation, is equally certain. He dedicates the three volumes of the 'Lady's Library' to three different ladies. Lady Burlington, Mrs. Boevey, and Mrs. Steele; he describes each of them in terms of the highest commendation, but each of them is distinguished by very discriminating characteristics. However exalted the characters of Lady Burlington, or Mrs. Steele, there is not one word in the dedication to either which corresponds to the character of the widow; but the characters of Mrs. Boevey and the Widow are drawn with marks of very striking coincidence. No. 113 of the *Spectator*, as far as it relates to the Widow is almost a parody on the character of Mrs. Boevey, as shown in the dedication. Sir ROGER tells his friend that she is a reading lady, and that her discourse was as learned as the best philosopher could possibly make. She reads upon the nature of plants, and understands everything. In the dedication Steele says, 'instead of assemblies and conversations, books and solitude have been your choice: you have charms of your own sex, and knowledge not inferior to the most learned of ours.' In No. 118, 'her superior merit is such,' says Sir ROGER, 'that I cannot approach her without awe, my heart is checked by too much esteem.' Dedication. 'Your person and fortune equally raise the admiration and awe of our whole sex.'

"She is described as having a Confidant, as the Knight calls her, to whom he expresses a peculiar aversion, No. 118 being chiefly on that subject. 'Of all persons,' says the good old Knight, 'be sure to set a mark on confidants.' I know not whether the lady was deserving of the Knight's reprobation, but Mrs. Boevey certainly had a female friend of this description, of the name of

Some Notes, &c.

Pope, who lived with her more than forty years, whom she left executrix, and who it is believed in the family did not execute her office in the most liberal manner."

The communication goes on to state that Mrs. Boevey's residence, Flaxley Abbey, was not far from the borders of Worcestershire; but that there was no tradition in the family of her having had such a law suit as is described by Sir ROGER. Indeed, a reference to dates shows such a circumstance to have been impossible, unless the phenomenon of a widow of nine years old could be credited. Mr. Boevey died in 1691, when his wife was twenty-two; now as the *Spectator* fixed the old Knight's age at fifty-six, and as Sir ROGER himself affirms that the Widow first "cast her bewitching eye upon him" in his twenty-third year, that fatal glance must have flashed in 1678, when Mrs. Boevey was in her girlhood. But this weighs not a feather in the scale of evidence; no true artist copies *every* trait of his subject, and the verisimilitude is not diminished because the Gloucestershire enslaver was younger and not so litigious as the Worcestershire enchantress.

Mrs. Boevey died January 21, 1726-7, in her 57th year, and was buried in the family vault at Flaxley with an inscription on the walls of the chapel to her memory. There is also a monument to her in Westminster Abbey, erected by her executrix.

Sir Roger's Widow will never die.

Chapter IX: The Coverley Economy
No. 114. Wednesday, July 11, 1711. By Steele.

Page 57. He would save four shillings in the Pound. The land tax; which from 1689 was continued by annual enactments, till Lowndes's act fixed it at 4*s.* in the pound. Gay addressed an epistle in verse "to my ingenious and worthy friend William Lowndes, esq. author of the celebrated treatise in folio called the land tax bill." Some of the lines run thus:—

> "Thy copious Preamble so smoothly runs,
> Taxes no more appear like Legal Duns,
> Lords, Knights, and Squires the Assessor's Power obey;
> We read with Pleasure though with Pain we pay."

The Coverley Papers

"Poets of Old had such a wondrous Power,
That with their Verses they could raise a tower;
But, in thy Prose, a greater Force is found—
What Poet ever raised Three Thousand Pound?"

In 1799 the land tax was made perpetual.

Chapter X: The Coverley Hunt
Nos. 115 and 116. Friday July 13, and Saturday 14, 1711.

The former paper is by Addison, the latter by Eustace Budgell.

Page 60. *Such a system of Tubes and Glands as has been before mentioned:*—viz. in the Commencement of No. 115. "I consider the Body as a system of Tubes and Glands, or to use a more Rustick Phrase, a Bundle of Pipes and Strainers, fitted to one another after so wonderful a manner as to make a proper Engine for the Soul to work with."

Page 66. *His stable Doors are patched with Noses that belonged to Foxes of the Knight's own hunting down.* Although the *Spectator* advocated in this, and other pages, moderate indulgence in the Sports of the Field, the excessive passion of Country Gentlemen for them, to the exclusion of more intellectual pastimes, he elsewhere deplores. In a later volume he quotes a saying that the curse fulminated by Goliah having missed David, had rested on the modern Squire:—"I will give thee to the fowls of the air, and to the beasts of the field." The Country Gentleman was respected by his neighbours, less for morality or intellect, than for the number of Foxes' noses he could show nailed to his stables and barns.

The sedentary, though assuredly less healthful and respectable games and pastimes introduced by Charles the Second and his followers from abroad, had not, even in Queen Anne's day, become so thoroughly naturalized as they were afterwards; and ladies keenly participated in the sports of the field. The Queen herself followed the hounds in a chaise with one horse, "which," says Swift, "she drives herself; and drives furiously, like Jehu; and is a mighty hunter, like Nimrod." She was, if Stella's journalist did not exaggerate, quite equal to runs even longer than

174

those performed by the Coverley hounds; for, on the 7th August, 1711, she drove before dinner five and forty miles after a stag.

Page 63. *Sir* Roger *has disposed of his Beagles and got a pack of Stop-hounds.* We infer from Blaine's Rural Sports, that when one of these hounds found the scent, he gave notice of his good fortune by deliberately squatting to impart more effect to his deep tones, and to get wind for a fresh start.

Page 66. *The Huntsman threw down his pole before the dogs.* The undrained, uncultivated condition of the country in Sir Roger's days, made hunting on horseback by no means so easy as it is at present. The master of the pack therefore could follow straighter over bogs, morasses, and ditches, on foot, than the squire could on horseback. To assist him in leaping, the pedestrian hunter used a pole. Some of the leaps taken in this manner would surprise an equestrian huntsman of the present day.

Page 64. *Sir* Roger *is so keen at this Sport, that he has been out almost every Day since I came here.* The *Spectator* arrived at Coverley Hall on one of the last days of June, and the hunt described in the paper dated as above is said to have taken place "yesterday." Mr. Budgell—who was the son of a Devonshire Esquire—ought to have known better than to make Sir Roger indulge in his favourite sport so decidedly out of season. It is a wonder how so grave a mistake escaped editorial revision.

Page 67. *The Lines out of Mr. Dryden*—occur in "An Epistle to his kinsman, J. Dryden, Esquire, of Chesterton."

Chapter XI: *The Coverley Witch*

No. 117. Saturday, July 14, 1711. By Addison.

Page 69. *The following description in Otway.* The lines quoted in the text are from the second Act of the Orphan.

Page 72. *I hear there is scarce a Village in England, that has not a Moll White.* The belief in witchcraft was in Anne's reign something more than merely popular. The act of James (Anno: 1. cap. 12) was in full force. By it death was decreed to whoever dealt with evil or wicked spirits, or invoked them whereby any persons were killed or lamed; or discovered where anything was hidden, or provoked unlawful love, &c. Under this law two

175

women were executed at Northampton just before the *Spectator* began to be published; and, not long after, (1716) a Mrs. Hicks and her daughter were hanged at Huntingdon for selling their souls to the devil, making their neighbours vomit pins, raising a storm so that a certain ship was "almost" lost, and a variety of other impossible crimes. By 1736 these superstitions abated; the Witch Act had become dormant; and, on an ignorant person attempting in that year to enforce it against an old woman in Surrey, it was repealed (10th Geo. II.)

Chapter XII: The Coverley Love Match
Spectator, No. 118. Monday, July 16, 1711. By Steele.

Chapter XIII: The Coverley Etiquette
No. 119. Tuesday, July 17, 1711. By Addison.

Page 82. *The women in many parts are still trying to vie with each other in the height of their head dresses.* This, at the date of the present paper, was being decidedly "behind the fashion:" for in 1711, the mode changed. Still the provincials had their excuses, for in No. 98, the *Spectator* affirms that there is no such variable thing in nature as a lady's head-dress: "Within my own Memory I have known it rise and fall above thirty Degrees. About ten years ago it shot up to a very great height, insomuch that the female part of our species were much taller than men. The women were of such an enormous stature, that we appeared as Grasshoppers before them: At present the whole sex is in a manner dwarfed and shrunk into a Race of Beauties that seems almost another species. I remember several ladies, who were once very near seven foot high, that at present want some inches of five: how they came to be thus curtailed I cannot learn."

Besides the numerous papers devoted to women's attire, the whole of No. 265 is a satire on the single subject of head-dresses. This frequent recurrence to the small absurdities of female fashion is said to have damaged the prosperity of the *Spectator*. Soon after the appearance of the above cited number, Swift writes impatiently in his Journal, "I will not meddle with the *Spectator:* let him *fair-sex* it to the world's end."

Some Notes, &c.

Chapter XIV: The Coverley Ducks

Nos. 120 and 121. Wednesday, July 18th, and Thursday, 19th, 1711. By Addison.

Chapter XV: Sir Roger on the Bench

Spectator, No. 122. Friday, July 20th, 1711. By Addison.

Page 89. *He is just within the Game Act.* The 3rd of James the First, chap. 14, clause v. provides that if any person who has not real property producing forty pounds per Ann.: or who has not two hundred pounds worth of goods and chattels, shall presume to shoot game; "Then any person having lands, tenements, or hereditaments, of the clear yearly value of one hundred pounds a year, may take from the person or possession of such malefactor or malefactors, and to his own use for ever keep, such guns, bows, cross-bows, buckstalls, engine-hays, nets, ferrets, and coney dogs, &c." This amiable enactment—which permitted a one-hundred-pound-freeholder to become in his single person, accuser, witness, judge, jury, and executioner; and which made an equally respectable but poorer man who shot a hare a "malefactor"—was the law of the land even so lately as 1827, for it was only repealed by the 7th and 8th Geo. IV. chap. 27.

Chapter XVI: The Story of an Heir

No. 123. Saturday, July 21, 1711. By Addison.

Page 95. *Eudoxus and Leontine began the world with small estates.*

"Being very well pleased with this day's *Spectator*, (writes Mr. Addison to Mr. Wortley, under date 'July 21, 1711'), I cannot forbear sending you one of them, and desiring your opinion of the story in it. When you have a son I shall be glad to be his Leontine, as my circumstances will probably be like his. I have within this twelve-month lost a place of 2000*l.* per annum, an estate in the Indies of 14,000*l.*, and what is worse than all the rest, my mistress. Hear this and wonder at my philosophy. I

177

find they are going to take away my Irish place from me too: to which I must add, that I have just resigned my fellowship, and that the stocks sink every day. If you have any hints or subjects, pray send me up a paper full. I long to talk an evening with you. I believe I shall not go to Ireland this summer, and perhaps would pass a month with you, if I knew where. Lady Bellasis is very much your humble servant. Dick Steele and I often remember you."

Of the estate in "the Indies"—referred to also by Swift—no intelligible notice has been found. The mistress was probably the perverse widow, the Countess; who, at that date, had perhaps cast him off "for ever"—after the manner of capricious ladies— several times during a single courtship.

Chapter XVII: Sir Roger and Party Spirit

Nos. 125 and 126. Wednesday, July 25th, and Thursday 26th, 1711. Both by Addison.

Page 101. *This worthy knight had occasion to enquire which was the way to St. Anne's lane.* There were two St. Anne's lanes which might have cost Sir ROGER trouble to find; one "on the north side of St. Martin's-le-Grand just within Aldersgate Street," (Stow); and the other—which it requires sharp eyes to find in Strype's map—turning out of Great Peter Street, Westminster. Mr. Peter Cunningham, in his admirable Hand Book for London, prefers supposing Sir ROGER enquiring his way in Westminster.

Page 102. Sir ROGER *generally closes his narrative with reflections on the Mischief that Parties do in the County.* There is scarcely a period when party spirit raged so fiercely as at the date of these numbers of the *Spectator;* for, although faction had long sheathed the sword, the tongue in coffee-houses and the pen in pamphlets were never more bitterly or rancorously employed. Only a few months previously, the trial of Dr. Sacheverel and the "bed-chamber cabal"—of which Mrs. Masham was chief—had overturned the Godolphin ministry; and had brought in the Tories with Harley at their head, backed by a new and eminently Tory House of Commons, with Whiggery enough in the Upper House and in the camarilla, to keep the flames of party in full glow.

Some Notes, &c.

So nearly were sides balanced in the House of Lords, that to carry the peace project, which ended in the treaty of Utrecht, Anne was afterwards obliged to make twelve new Tory Peers— a "jury" of such well packed Tories, that a Whig wit asked one of them if they intended to vote by their "foreman." The Duchess of Somerset was still retained about the person of the Queen; and counteracted, in part, the subtle Tory whisperings of Mrs. Masham into Anne's ear. The lucrative employments of the Duchess of Marlborough were divided between these two favourites The Duke was on the eve of being impeached for peculation, and his regiment had actually been transferred to Hill, Mrs. Masham's brother. The Whigs violently advocated the continuance of a war which Marlborough's victories had made at once so profitable to his private fortune and so glorious to the nation. The Tories and the Queen strove equally for peace: nor did this contest suspend the Church controversy which Sacheverel's trial had brought to issue without deciding.

These questions ranged the British Public into two ranks, under Whig and Tory banners; and carried the battle into private life in the manner not less truthfully than humorously described in the text, and in various other chapters of the *Spectator*. Families were estranged and friendships broken up, especially amongst those who played prominent parts in the struggle—such as Swift on the Tory, and Addison and Steele on the Whig side. Yet it is gratifying to observe, that the softening influences of literature afforded a lingering link of union to these men even after they were in political opposition. Swift, the foremost party pamphleteer of his day, did not scruple to use his influence with Harley, in favour of "Pastoral" Philips, Congreve, and on one occasion for Steele. On the day of publication of the paper which forms part of our present chapter (Thursday, July 26th, 1711), Swift, Addison, and Steele, dined together at young Jacob Tonson's, "Mr. Addison and I talked as usual, and as if we had seen one another yesterday; and Steele and I were very easy, though I wrote him a biting letter in answer to one of his, where he desired me to recommend a friend of his to the Lord Treasurer."

Again, under a later date, Swift writes to Stella, "I met Pastoral Philips and Mr. Addison on the Mall to-day, and took a turn with them; but they looked terribly dry and cold. A curse on Party!"

The bonds of other classes of society were more forcibly riven. The lower the grade the more inveterate the contention: for, as Pope said about that time, "There never was any party, faction, sect, or cabal whatsoever, in which the most ignorant were not the most violent; for a bee is not a busier animal than a blockhead." Even trade was tainted by the poison of party. The buying, in its dealings with the selling public, more generally enquired into the political principles of tradesmen, than into the excellence or defects of their wares. Inn-keepers as we find in the text were especially subjected to this rule, and their politics were known by the signs at their doors. Addison's "Freeholder's" introduction to the Tory fox-hunter was commenced by the recommendation of a host—"A lusty fellow, that lives well, is at least three yards in the girt, and is the best Church of England man upon the road."

Not the least conspicuous partizans were, alas, of the gentler sex; for the chiefs of each faction were women, and their theatre of war the Queen's bedchamber. The petty expedients of each faction to distinguish itself in public from the other, are happily ridiculed in various parts of the *Spectator*. At the play Whig and Tory ladies sat at opposite sides of the house, and "patched" on opposite sides of their faces:—"I must here take notice, that *Rosalinda*, a famous Whig partizan, has most unfortunately a very beautiful Mole on the Tory part of her forehead; which being very conspicuous, has occasioned many mistakes, and given an handle to her enemies to misrepresent her face, as though it had revolted from the Whig interest. But whatever this natural patch may seem to insinuate, it is well known that her notions of government are still the same. This unlucky Mole, however, has misled several coxcombs; and like the hanging out of false colours, made some of them converse with *Rosalinda* in what they thought the spirit of her party, when on a sudden she has given them an unexpected fire, that has sunk them all at once. If *Rosalinda* is unfortunate in her Mole, *Nigranilla* is as unhappy in a Pimple, which forces her, against her inclination, to patch on the Whig side." No. 81.

So angry were the Whig ladies with the Queen when she presented Prince Eugene with the jewelled sword, that they abstained in a body from appearing at Court on that occasion:—which being that of Her Majesty's birthday was evidence of unprecedented party rancour.

Chapter XVIII: The Coverley Gipseys
No. 130. Monday, July 30th, 1711. By Addison.

Chapter XIX: A Summons to London
Spectator, No. 131. Tuesday, July 31st, 1711. By Addison.

Page 112. *What they here call a White Witch.* According to popular belief, there were three classes of Witches;—White, Black, and Gray. The first helped, but could not hurt; the second the reverse, and the third did both. White Spirits caused stolen goods to be restored; they charmed away diseases, and did other beneficent acts; neither did a little harmless mischief lie wholly out of their way:—Dryden says

"At least as little honest as he could,
And like White Witches mischievously good."

Chapter XX: The Journey from Coverley Hall
No. 132. Wednesday, August 1, 1711. By Steele.

Page 115. *As soon as we arrived at the Inn, the Servant enquired of the Chamberlain what Company he had for the Coach?* The best possible illustration of this passage is Hogarth's print of the Inn yard. The landlady in her semicircular glass case, or penthouse bar; the parting drams being imbibed by the coachman and by some of the leave-takers; the sleepiness of the ostlers and porters, and the deliberation of the passengers show how a journey was then commenced. The enquiry made by the servant was usual. It was a pardonable curiosity in the Spectator to try and learn with whom he was to be jumbled over rugged roads for the three entire days which were consumed by a stage coach in a single transit from Worcester to London.

Although it was more than a half century later before any

great advance in road-making took place, yet the dawn of improvement in carriages was just beginning to break. To the *Spectator* for June 24, 1711, is appended the following advertisement: "Whereas Her Majesty has been graciously pleased lately to grant Letters Patent to Henry Mill, Gent. for the Sole Use and Benefit of making and vending certain Steel Springs by him invented for the Ease of Persons riding in Chaises, &c. They effectually prevent all Jolts on Kennels and Rugged Ways."

Page 116. *The Captain's Half-Pike.* The soldier's pike had been recently superseded by the socket bayonet. Noncommissioned officers however retained the halbert, and officers their half-pike. The Duke of Monmouth is described at the battle of Sedgemoor as having rushed about on foot among his broken levies to encourage them "pike in hand."

Page 118. *Our Reckonings, Apartments and Accommodation fell under Ephraim.* This duty was rather onerous, on account of the number of stoppages on the road, the consequent multiplicity of reckonings, and the equal number of attempts at overcharge. It was the custom for the male to pay for the refreshments of the female passengers. This was often felt as a grievous tax, and was in some cases resisted. Thoresby, recording in his diary a stage-coach journey from Wakefield to London in 1714, states that on the third day there was an accession of passengers, "which though Females, were more chargeable in Wine and Brandy than the former Part of the journey, wherein we had neither; but the Next Day we gave them Leave to Treat Themselves."

Page 119. *The right we had of taking Place as going to London, of all Vehicles coming from thence.* This rule of the road was occasioned by the bad condition of the public ways. On the best lines of communication ruts were so deep and obstructions so formidable that it was only in fine weather that the whole breadth of the road was available, for on each side was often a quagmire of mud. Seldom could two vehicles pass each other unless one of them stopped. Which that should be caused endless disputes, and not a few accidents. Some obstinate drivers preferred disputation, and even collision and broken wheels or broken bones, to "pulling up" in deference to a rival Jehu. At such times the path was blocked up for hours, and when an accumulation of vehicles was the consequence, the end was a general fight amongst the carriers, carters, and coachmen.—Single combat also arose, from a like cause, among pedestrians in the streets to settle the important question of who should "take the wall." This was a real privilege when, in ordinary weather, the edge of the footpath was heaped with mud; and, on wet days, streams poured upon it from the eaves of the houses.

Chapter XXI: Sir Roger in London
No. 269. Tuesday, January 8, 1712. By Addison.

Page 121. *He told me that his Master was come up to get a Sight of Prince Eugene.* The Prince's mission to this country was no less popular than his victories—gained in association with Marlborough—had made his person. It was to urge the prosecution with Austria of the war against France in terms of the treaty of 1706, and to endeavour to restore to the Queen's favour his great ally the Duke, who had only four days before his arrival been dismissed with disgrace from all his employments. "Gratitude, esteem, the parnership in so many military operations," we read in Prince Eugene's Autobiography, "and pity for a person in disgrace, caused me to throw myself with emotion into Marlborough's arms."

Nothing could exceed the enthusiastic reception with which Eugene was greeted; and, an adroit illustration of the eagerness of the public to behold him, is the bringing Sir ROGER up to London solely for that purpose, only two days after the Prince's appearance. "The knight," says the *Spectator*, "made me promise to get him a stand in some convenient place where he might have a full view of that extraordinary man." This was in fact a necessity; for whenever the Prince ventured in the streets, he was beset by eager multitudes, from the evening of his arrival (5th January, 1712) till his departure.

While there was a chance of gaining over the illustrious envoy, the Court party joined in the general homage, and on her birth-day, Anne gave the Prince a jewelled sword, valued at £4,500. *Then* Swift, at first sight, "didn't think him an ugly faced fellow, but well enough; and a good shape." (*Journal,*

Jan. 13.) Eugene was not to be won; and persisted in passing most of his time with Marlborough: whom Harley, the lord treasurer, had just stripped of his title of general. One day at dinner, while Harley was plying the Prince with flattery and depreciating Marlborough, he called Eugene the *first* General in Europe. "If I am so," said the prince, "'tis to your lordship I am indebted for the distinction." Both by words and behaviour, therefore, Prince Eugene firmly adhered to the cause he had come over to advance, and he fell into utter disrepute with the Tory or peace party. Then it was that Swift, eager as the rest, got a second glimpse of the great man; but the same pair of eyes jaundiced with party prejudice found him "plaguy yellow and literally ugly besides." (*Journal*, Feb. 10.)

Meanwhile the illustrious Envoy was the idol of the populace and of the Whigs. He returned their idolatry by a pleasing affability while in public; and by a variety of small but agreeable courtesies in private. Amongst these it must be noted that he stood sponsor to Steele's second son. The Whig ladies professed to be in love with him, and returned a compliment often paid to themselves by making him their toast. In company, he had, according to Burnet, "a most unaffected modesty, and does scarcely bear the acknowledgements that all the world pay him."

His popularity was gall to the Tories, who with a too-prevalent and mean revenge set about showering libels upon him On the 17th of March, Prince Eugene retired from this country: his disgust and disappointment slightly tempered by the kindness of the Queen; who, at parting, gave him her portrait.

A running fire of squibs and pamphlets was kept up against the Tories on account of their cringing reception, and spiteful dismissal of the illustrious visitor. One was advertised in No. 471 of the *Spectator* as "Prince Eugene not the Man you took him for; or a Merry Tale of a Modern Hero. Price 6*d*."

Page 122. "*I was no sooner come into Grays-Inn Walks, but I heard my Friend upon the Terrace hemming twice or thrice to himself, for he loves to clear his Pipes in good Air.*" Gray's Inn Gardens formed for a long time a fashionable promenade. The chief entrance to them was Fulwood's Rents, now a pent-up retreat for squalid poverty; yet, in Sir ROGER's day, no place was better adapted for "clearing his pipes in good air," for scarcely a house intervened thence to Hampstead. A contemporary satirist (but who can scarcely be quoted without an apology) affords a graphic description of this promenade;—"I found none but a parcel of Superannuated Debauchees huddled up in Cloaks, Frieze Coats, and Wadded Gowns, to preserve their old Carcasses from the Sharpness of Hampstead Air; creeping up and down in Pairs and Leashes no faster than the Hand of a Dial or a County Convict going to Execution: some talking of Law, some of Religion, and some of Politics.—After I had taken two or three Turns round, I sat myself down in the Upper Walk, where just before me on a Stone Pedestal was fixed an old rusty Horizontal Dial with the Gnomon broke short off." Round this sundial seats were arranged in a semi-circle.

Gray's Inn Gardens were resorted to by less reputable characters than the beggar whom good Sir ROGER scolded and relieved. Expert pickpockets and plausible ring-droppers found easy prey there on crowded days. In the plays of the period, Gray's Inn Gardens are frequently mentioned as a place of assignation for clandestine lovers.

Page 124. *The late Act of Parliament for securing the Church of England.* The 10th Anne, Cap. 2. "An Act for preserving the Protestant Religion by better securing the Church of England as by law established," &c. It was known popularly as the act of "Occasional Conformity."

Page 125. *The Pope's Procession.* Each anniversary of Queen Elizabeth's accession (Nov. 17) was for many years celebrated by the citizens of London in a manner expressive of their detestation of the Church of Rome. A procession—at times sufficiently attractive for royal spectators—paraded the principal streets, the chief figure being an effigy of

"The Pope, that Pagan full of pride,"

well executed in wax and expensively adorned with robes and a tiara. He was accompanied by a train of cardinals and jesuits; and at his ear stood a buffoon in the likeness of a horned devil. After having been paraded through divers streets, His Holiness was exultingly burnt opposite to the Whig club near the Temple gate in Fleet Street. After the discovery of the Rye House plot, the Pope's procession was discontinued; but was resuscitated on the acquittal of the seven bishops and dethronement of James II. Sacheverel's trial had added a new interest to the ceremony; and on the occasion referred to by Sir ROGER, besides a popular dread of the Church being—from the listlessness of the Ministers and the machinations of the Pretender—in danger, there was a very general opposition to the peace with France, for which the Tories were intriguing. The party cry of "No peace" was shouted in the same breath with "No popery."

The Whigs were determined, it was said, to give significance and force to these watchwords by getting up the anniversary show of 1711 with unprecedented splendour. No good Protestant, no honest hater of the French could refuse to subscribe his guinea for such an object; and it was said, upwards of a thousand pounds were collected for the effigies and their dresses and decorations alone; independent of a large fund for incidental expenses. The Pope, the Devil, and the Pretender were, it was reported, fashioned in the likeness of the obnoxious Cabinet Ministers. The procession was to take place at night, and "a thousand mob" were, it was asserted, to be hired to carry flambeaux at a crown a piece, and as much beer and brandy as would inflame them for mischief. The pageant was to open with "twenty-four bagpipes marching four and four, and playing the memorable tune of Lillibullero." Presently was to come "a figure representing Cardinal Gaulteri, (lately made by the Pretender protector of the English nation), looking down on the ground in sorrowful posture; "his train supported by two missionaries from Rome, supposed to be now in England."—"Two pages throwing beads, bulls, pardons, and indulgences."—"Two jack puddings sprinkling holy-water."—"Twelve hautboys playing the 'Greenwood tree.'"—Then were to succeed "Six beadles with protestant flails," and after a variety of other satirical mummers the grand centre piece was to show itself:—"The pope under a magnificent canopy, with a right silver fringe, accompanied by the Chevalier St. George on the left and his councellor the devil on his right." The whole procession was to close with twenty streamers displaying this couplet wrought on each,

Some Notes, &c.

"God bless Queen Anne, the nation's great defender,
Keep out the French, the Pope, and the Pretender."

To be ready for this grand Spectacle the figures were deposited at a house in Drury Lane, whence the procession was to march ("with proper reliefs of lights at several stations") to St. James's Square, thence through Pall Mall, the Strand, Drury Lane, and Holborn to Bishopsgate Street, and return through St. Paul's Church Yard to the Bonfire in Fleet Street. "After proper ditties were sung, the Pretender was to have been committed to the flames, being first absolved by the Cardinal Gaulteri. After that the said cardinal was to be absolved by the Pope and burnt. And then the devil was to jump into the flames with his holiness in his arms."

According, however, to the Tories, who spread the most exaggerated reports of these preparations, there were to have been certain accidents which were duly and deliberately contrived beforehand by the conspirators. Besides the great conflagration of the Sovereign Pontiff, there was to have been several supplementary bonfires in the line of march, into which certain actors of the show were to fling a mock copy of the preliminary articles of peace. This was to be the signal for a general exclamation of "No peace!" Horse messengers had also been engaged—so wrote the Cabinet scribes—to gallop into the crowd "as if to break their necks, their hacks all foam" to cry out *the Queen is dead at Hampton Court!*" Lord Wharton and several noblemen of even higher rank were to disguise themselves as sailors, to mix with and incite the mob. But the grand stroke was to be dealt by the Duke of Marlborough. He was on his way from Flanders—covered, most inopportunely for his enemies, with the glory of one of his best achievements; that of having passed the strongly fortified lines drawn by the French from Bouchain to Arras. On this famous eve the duke was to have made his entry through Aldgate, and there met with the cry of "Victory, Bouchain, the Lines, no Peace!"

But all this was harmless as compared with the threatened sequel. On the diabolical programme were said to be inscribed certain houses that were to be burnt down. That of the Commissioners of Accounts in Essex Street was to form the first pyre, because in it had been discovered and completed Marlborough's commissarial defalcations. The lord treasurer's was to follow. Harley himself was to have been torn to pieces, as the Dutch pensionary De Witt had been. Indeed the entire city was only to have escaped destruction and rapine by a miracle. It is here that the *Spectator* himself comes upon the scene. "The *Spectator* who ought to be but a looker on, was to have been an assistant; that, seeing London in a flame, he might have opportunity to paint after the life, and remark the behaviour of the people in the ruin of their country; so to have made a diverting *Spectator*."

These were the coarse excuses which the Tories put forth for spoiling the show. At midnight on the 16-17th of Nov. a posse of Constables made forcible entry into the Drury Lane temple of the waxen images, and by force of arms seized the Pope, the Pretender, the Cardinals, the Devil and all his works, a chariot to have been drawn by six of his imps, the canopies, the bagpipes, the bulls, the pardons, the Protestant flails, the streamers,—in short the entire paraphernalia. At one fell swoop the whole collection was carried off to the Cock pit at Whitehall, then the privy Council office. That the city apprentices should not be wholly deprived of their expected treat, fifteen of the group were exhibited to the public gratis. "I saw to-day the Pope, the Devil, and the other figures of cardinals, &c. fifteen in all, which have made such a noise. I hear the owners of them are so impudent, that their design is to replace them by law. The images are not worth forty pounds, so I stretched a little when I said a thousand. The Grub Street account of that tumult is published. The devil is not like Lord Treasurer; they were all in your odd antic masks bought in common shops." Thus wrote Swift to Stella; yet to the public he either gave, or superintended an account of the affair which was simply a string of all the mendacious exaggerations then wilfully put about by his patrons. Such were the party tactics of Sir Roger's time.

Page 125. *Squire's Coffee House*. In Fulwood's Rents, leading from Holborn into Gray's Inn Gardens as mentioned ante. It was much frequented by the Benchers and Students of Gray's Inn. Squire was a "noted coffee man" who died in 1717.

Some Notes, &c.

Chapter XXII: Sir Roger in Westminster Abbey
Spectator, No. 329. Tuesday, March 18, 1712. By Addison.

Page 127. *He had been reading my paper upon Westminster Abbey.* Spectator, No. 26.

Page 127. *He called for a Glass of the Widow Trueby's Water.* One of the innumerable "strong waters" drunk, it is said (perhaps libellously) chiefly by the fair sex as an exhilarant; the excuses being the cholic and "the vapours." Addison, who pretends in the text to find it unpalatable, is accused of having been a constant imbiber of the Widow's distillations. Indeed, Tyers goes so far as to say on the authority of "Tacitus" Gordon, that Addison hastened his end by indulgence in them. Although an advertisement of these waters is not to be found in the Folio *Spectator*, yet the curious will see in it strong puffs of other potent spirits in disguise—thanks probably to the business connexions of Mr. Lillie, perfumer. A "grateful electuary" is recommended in No. 113 as having the power of raising the spirits, of curing loss of memory, and revivifying all the noble powers of the soul,—at the small charge of two and sixpence per bottle.

Another chymical secret, in No. 120, promises to cure "the vapours in women, infallibly, in an instant." Daffy's Elixir is advertised in No. 356.

Page 128. *The Sickness being at Dantzick.*—The plague which raged there in 1709. "Idleness which has long raged in the world, destroys more in every great town than the plague has done at Dantzic." *Tatler*, Nov. 22, 1709.

Page 129. *"Sir Cloudesly Shovel! a very gallant Man."* This monument is in the south aisle of the choir.

"*Sir Cloudesly Shovel's* Monument has very often given me great Offence: Instead of the brave rough *English* Admiral, which was the distinguishing Character of that plain gallant Man, he is represented on his Tomb by the Figure of a Beau, dressed in a long Perriwig, and reposing himself upon Velvet Cushions under a Canopy of State. The Inscription is answerable to the Monument; for instead of celebrating the many remarkable Actions he had performed in the Service of his Country, it acquaints us only with the Manner of his Death, in which it was impossible for him to reap any Honour." *Spectator*, No. 26.

The Sculptor was F. Bird. Sir Cloudesly Shovel died in 1707.

Page 129. *Dr. Busby! a great Man—he whipp'd my Grandfather*. Dr. Busby was head master of Westminster School for Fifty-five years, and had the credit of having furnished both the church and the state with a greater number of eminent scholars than any other pedagogue. At the Restoration he was made a prebendary of Westminster, and carried the sacred ampulla at the Coronation of Charles the Second. He was eighty-nine years old when he died in 1695. His monument, sculptured by Bird, stands not far from that of Sir Cloudesly Shovel.

Page 130. *The Statesman Cecil upon his Knees*. In the chapel of St. Nicholas. This tomb was erected by the great Lord Burleigh, in the reign of Queen Elizabeth, to the memory of his wife Mildred and their daughter Anne whose effigies lie under a carved arch. "At the base of the monument, within Corinthian columns, are kneeling figures of Sir Robert Cecil, their son, and three grand-daughters. The inscription is in Latin, very long and very tiresome." *Peter Cunningham's Westminster Abbey*.

Page 130. *That Martyr to good Housewifery who died with the prick of a Needle*. This is one of the "hundred lies" which the attendant is said to have told Goldsmith's Citizen of the World "without blushing." The monument, in St. Edmund's Chapel, is that of Elizabeth, youngest daughter of Lord John Russel (temp. 1584). "The figure is melancholily inclining her Cheek to her Right Hand, and with the Fore-finger of her Left directing us to behold the Death's Head placed at her Feet." (*Keepe Monas. Westm.*) This alone is said to have originated an unwarrantable verdict of "died from the prick of a needle."

Page 130. *The Stone was called Jacob's Pillar [pillow]*. This is the stone or "Marble fatal Chair" which Gathelus, son of Cecrops King of Athens, is said to have sent from Spain with his son when he invaded Ireland; and which Fergus son of Gyric won there and conveyed to Cove. The stone was set into a chair in which the kings of Scotland were crowned, till Edward the first offered it, with other portions of the Scottish Regalia, at the shrine of Edward the Confessor as an evidence of his absolute

Some Notes, &c.

conquest of Scotland. A Leonine Couplet was cut in the stone which has been thus translated:

"The Scots shall brook that Realm as native ground
(If Weirds fail not) wherever this stone is found."

This prophecy was fulfilled, to the satisfaction of the faithful in prophecy, by the accession of James VI. to the English Crown. How it got the name of Jacob's pillow is difficult to trace. It is a piece of common rough Scotch sandstone; and Sir ROGER's question was extremely pertinent.—The other coronation chair was placed in the Abbey in the reign of William and Mary.

Page 130. *Sir* ROGER, *in the next Place, laid his hand upon Edward the Third's Sword.* This, "The monumental sword that conquered France," is placed with his shield near the tomb of Edward, and which he caused to be carried before him in France. The sword is seven feet long and weighs eighteen pounds.

Page 131. *The Figure of one of our English Kings without a Head.* The effigy of Henry V. which was plated with silver except the head, and that was of solid metal. At the dissolution of the monasteries the figure was stripped of its plating, and the head stolen.

Chapter XXIII: Sir Roger at the Play

Spectator, No. 335. Tuesday, March 25, 1712. By Addison.

Page 133. *He had a great Mind to see the new Tragedy.* This was the Distressed Mother by Ambrose, otherwise "Pastoral" Philips; and, as it was advertised in the above number of the *Spectator* to be performed for the sixth time, Sir ROGER must be supposed to have witnessed its fifth performance. The "first night" is thus announced in the *Spectator* and in the *Daily Courant* of 17th March, 1712,

"By Desire of several Ladies of Quality; by Her Majesty's Company of Comedians:

"At the Theatre Royal, Drury Lane, this present Monday being 17th March will be presented a new Tragedy called

The Coverley Papers

"THE DISTRESSED MOTHER,

"(By Her Majesty's Command no person will be admitted behind the scenes.)

"Pyrrhus, Mr. Booth.   Andromache, Mrs. Oldfield.
Phœnix, Mr. Bowman.   Cephisa, Mrs. Knight.
Orestes, Mr. Powell.   Hermione, Mrs. Porter.
Pylades, Mr. Mills.   Cleone, Mrs. Cox."

Addison had a strong friendship for Philips, and took extraordinary pains, first to get his friend's play upon the Stage, and next to make it succeed; for, according to Spence he caused the house to be packed on the first night. No. 290 of the *Spectator* opens with a puff preliminary:

"The Players, who know I am very much their Friend, take all Opportunities to express a Gratitude to me for being so. They could not have a better Occasion of obliging me, than one which they lately took hold of. They desired my Friend WILL HONEYCOMB to bring me to the Reading of a new Tragedy, it is called *The Distressed Mother*. I must confess, tho' some Days are passed since I enjoyed that Entertainment, the Passions of the several Characters dwell strongly upon my Imagination; and I congratulate the Age, that they are at last to see Truth and humane Life represented in the Incidents which concern Heroes and Heroines. The Stile of the Play is such as becomes those of the first Education, and the Sentiments worthy those of the highest Figure. It was a most exquisite Pleasure to me, to observe real Tears drop from the Eyes of those who had long made it their Profession to dissemble affliction: and the Player, who read, frequently threw down the Book till he had given Vent to the Humanity which rose in him at some irresistible Touches of the imagined Sorrow."

Whoever dips into this turgid translation of Racine's Andromache will be much amused at the green-room grief it is said to have drawn forth. Like many a worse play, some of its success was occasioned by the Epilogue as delivered by Mrs. Oldfield. "This was the most successful composition of the kind ever yet," says Johnson, "spoken on the English theatre. The three first nights it was recited twice; and not only continued to be demanded through the run, as it is termed, of the play; but whenever it is recalled to the stage where by peculiar fortune, though a copy from the French, it keeps its place, the Epilogue is still expected and still spoken." Its reputed author was BUDGELL; but when Addison was asked how such a silly fellow could write so well? he replied, "The Epilogue was quite another thing when I saw it first." Tonson published the play; and when it was first printed, Addison's name appeared to the Epilogue; but happening to come into the shop early in the morning when the copies were to be issued, he ordered the credit of it to be given to Budgell, "that it might add weight to the solicitation which he was then making for a place." This story was told to Garrick by a member of the Tonson family.—The prologue was by Steele.

Page 133. *The Committee—a good Church-of-England Play*. This comedy, written by Sir Robert Howard, was popular so early as 1663. Pepys, in his diary of that year, under June 12 writes—"To the Theatre Royal, and there saw *The Committee*, a merry but indifferent play; only Lacy's part, an Irish Footman, is beyond imagination." Posterity has not ratified Pepys's criticism as to the "indifference" of *The Committee*, for it kept possession of the stage in one form or another till very lately. The part of Teague was always the greatest favourite, and gave to the Comedy the second title of "The Faithful Irishman." After Lacy it was filled with most applause by Leigh, whom Charles the Second called "*his* Comedian:" Griffin and Bowman respectively succeeded to it, and then the sponsor of the well-known jest book, Joe Miller; of whom a mezzotint likeness as Teague is still extant. *The Committee*, cut down to a farce, was till lately played under the title of *Honest Thieves*.

Much of its earlier celebrity was due to the political allusions in which *The Committee* abounds—to its being, in the words of Sir ROGER, "a good Church-of-England Play." Sir R. Howard wrote it to satirize, in the character of Obadiah, the proceedings of the Roundheads; and, at the faintest dawn of religious excitement its announcement in the play-bills was, even in Sir ROGER's time, sure to attract large audiences. Some five-and-twenty years before, when James the Second attempted to inflict popery upon Oxford, an interpolation by Leigh—who was playing Teague in that city—caused an intense commotion. The head of University College, Walker, (whose first name was the same as that of the chief part in the play—Obadiah) had gone so far, in obedience to the wishes of the king, as to introduce popish rites, and to turn his college into a Catholic seminary. This brought upon him great indignation, a tremendous burst of which was vented after Leigh's exploit:—towards the end of the Comedy Teague has to haul in Obadiah with a halter about his neck and to threaten to hang him for refusing to drink the king's health. "Here," says Colley Cibber, "Leigh to justify his purpose with a stronger provocation, put himself into a more than ordinary heat with his captive; and, having heightened his master's curiosity to know what Obadiah had done to deserve such usage, Leigh, folding his arms with a ridiculous stare of astonishment, replied: 'Upon my shoul, he has shange his religion!'" The allusion was caught up and ran round like wild fire; the theatre was suddenly in an uproar of applause. The play was stopped. Some of the audience rushed from the theatre, in open riot, to revile Obadiah Walker under his own windows. Afterwards lampoons abounded, and satirical ballads were publickly sung: the most popular of which began:—

"Old Obadiah
Sings Ave Maria."

This adventure was the first intimation the king received of the disaffection of his Oxford subjects to the popish proceedings he had set on foot there. He caused Leigh to be severely reprimanded; and, for fear of the worst, sent down a regiment of dragoons to keep the Protestant "town and gown" in check. It is not impossible that Addison may have assisted in this riot; for he had entered as a student at Queen's College about a year before it happened.

Page 133. *Would there not be some Danger on coming home late, in case the Mohocks should be abroad?* It had been for many previous years the favourite amusement of dissolute young men to form themselves into clubs and associations for the cow-

Some Notes, &c.

ardly pleasure of fighting and sometimes maiming harmless pedestrians, and even defenceless women. They took various slang designations. At the Restoration they were Muns and Tityre-Tus; then Hectors and Scourers; later still, Nickers (whose expensive delight it was to smash windows with showers of halfpence), Hawkabites, and lastly Mohocks. These last took their title from "a sort of cannibals in India who subsist by plundering and devouring all the nations about them." Nor was the designation inapt; for if there was one sort of brutality on which they prided themselves more than another, it was in tattooing; or slashing people's faces with, as Gay wrote, "new-invented wounds."

Some of their other exploits were quite as savage as those of their predecessors, although they aimed at dashing their mischief with wit and originality. They began the evening at their clubs, by drinking to excess in order to inflame what little courage they possessed. They then sallied forth sword in hand. Some enacted the part of "dancing masters" by thrusting their rapiers between the legs of sober citizens in such a fashion as to make them cut the most grotesque capers. The Hunt spoken of by Sir Roger was commenced by a "view hallo!" and as soon as the savage pack had run down their victim, they surrounded him, to form a circle with the points of their swords. One gave him a puncture in the rear which naturally made him wheel about, then came a prick from another, and so they kept him spinning like a top till in their mercy they chose to let him go free. An adventure of this kind is narrated in No. 332 of the *Spectator*.

Another savage diversion was thrusting women into barrels and rolling them down Snow or Ludgate hill: Gay sings

"———————————— their Mischiefs done
Wherefrom Snow Hill black sleepy torrents run;
How Matrons hoop'd within a Hogshead's Womb
Were tumbled furious thence; the falling Tomb
O'er the Stones thunders; bounds from Side to Side:
So Regulus to save his Country dy'd."

At the date of the present *Spectator* the outrages of the Mohocks were so intolerable that they became the subject of a

The Coverley Papers

Royal Proclamation issued on the 18th March, just a week before Sir ROGER's visit to Drury Lane. Swift—who was horribly afraid of them—mentions some of their villainies. He writes two days previously that "Two of the Mohocks caught a Maid of old Lady Winchelsea's at the Door of her House in the Park with a Candle and had just lighted out Somebody. They cut all her Face, and beat her without any Provocation."

The proclamation had little effect. On the very day after our party went to the play, we find Swift exclaiming—"They go on still, and cut people's faces every night! but they shan't cut mine;—I like it better as it is."

Page 134. *The same Sword that he made use of at the Battle of Steenkirk.* This battle was remarkable in the annals of fashion for giving the name to a modish neck-cloth. At the beginning of August, 1692, while William the Third was in Flanders at the head of the allies, he discovered an enemy's spy in his camp, and to facilitate a project of surprising the French, his majesty caused him to give his master false information. The king then set upon the enemy at day-break while they were still asleep, and routed them.

The French generals however rallied and formed their troops on favourable ground, turned the tables, and finally conquered. The allies were so crest-fallen and disunited by this defeat that William broke up the campaign and retired to England. The French were as much elated. Their generals—amongst whom were the Prince de Condé and the Duke de Vendôme—were received in Paris with acclamation and the roads were lined with jubilants. The *petits maîtres* shared in the general exultation, and although at that time it was their pride to arrange their lace cravats with the utmost elaboration and care; yet, when they heard of the disordered dress in which the generals appeared in the fight from their haste to get into it, they suddenly changed the fashion, and wore a sort of lace negligé, which they called a "Steinkirk." The fashion soon extended to England, and for several years the "Steinkirk" was your fop's only wear.

Chapter XXIV: Will Honeycomb on Widows
No. 359. Tuesday, April 22nd, 1712. By Budgell.

Some Notes, &c.

Chapter XXV: Sir Roger at Vauxhall
No. 383. Tuesday, May 20, 1712. By Addison.

Page 139. *I had promised to go with him on the Water to Spring-Garden.* Fox-hall or Vauxhall Gardens were a substitute for Old Spring Gardens, Charing Cross, when the latter ceased to be a place of public entertainment and began to be covered with private residences. The name was derived from a "Spring" which supplied a jet "by a wheel, which the gardener turns at a distance, through a number of little pipes." (*Hentzner's Travels.*) The jet was concealed and did not spurt forth until an unwary visitor trod on a particular spot, when there came a self-administered shower bath. This, with archery, bowls, a grove of "warbling birds," a pleasant yard and a pond for bathing furnished the amusements. "Sometimes," says Evelyn, "they would have music, and sup on barges on the water."

At the Restoration builders invaded Spring Gardens, and its name was transferred to Vauxhall Gardens, which formed part of the estate of Sir Samuel Morland, who had already (in 1667) built a large room there. Except the Spring the amusements were nearly the same as in the old garden. The "close walks" were an especial attraction for other reasons than the nightingales, which, in their proper season, warbled in the trees. "The windings and turnings in the little wilderness," quoth Tom Brown, "are so intricate, that the most experienced mothers have often lost themselves in looking for their daughters." We hear little of Vauxhall from the year of Sir ROGER's visit (1712) till 1732, when it was resuscitated by Mr. Jonathan Tyers: he termed it *Ridotto al Fresco*, collected an efficient orchestra, set up an organ, engaged Hogarth and Roubillác to decorate the great room with paintings and statuary, and issued silver season tickets at a guinea each. From his time till about ten or fifteen years since Vauxhall retained its popularity.

Page 141. *A great deal of the like Thames ribaldry.* The "silent highway" was peculiarly favourable for that interchange of wit and repartee in which the lower orders, and even facetious people of quality, loved to indulge. Taylor, the water poet, Swift,

197

and Dr. Johnson have bequeathed to us some of these smart sayings; but they are too coarse for repetition.

Chapter XXVI: Sir Roger Passeth Away

Spectator, No. 517. Thursday, Oct. 23, 1712. By Addison.

Page 148. *To keep them no longer in suspense,* Sir ROGER DE COVERLEY *is Dead.* "Mr. Addison was so fond of this character that a little before he laid down the *Spectator* (foreseeing that some nimble gentleman would catch up his pen the moment he quitted it) he said to our intimate friend with a certain warmth in his expression, which he was not often guilty of, 'I'll kill Sir ROGER that nobody else may murder him.'" *The Bee*, p. 26.

On this Chalmers sensibly remarks that "the killing of Sir ROGER has been sufficiently accounted for, without supposing that Addison despatched him in a fit of anger; for the work was about to close, and it appeared necessary to close the club; but whatever difference of opinion there may be concerning this circumstance, it is universally agreed that it produced a paper of transcendent excellence in all the graces of simplicity and pathos. There is not in our language any assumption of character more faithful than that of the honest butler; nor a more irresistible stroke of nature than the circumstance of the book received by Sir Andrew Freeport."

Budgell's story is another version of the reason Cervantes gave for killing *his* hero;—*para mi sola nacio Don Quixote, y yo para el.* Shakespere's motive for the early demise of Mercutio in the tragedy of Romeo and Juliet has been accounted for by a similar fiction.